Every Voice Should be Heard…
My Journey to Becoming an Advocate

ISBN: 979-8-9896045-6-2

Book Layout and Cover Page:
Caroline Blochlinger (cbadvertising.com)

Printed in the USA

COPYRIGHT PERMISSIONS

The following agencies or websites gave me their express permission
to quote their written material for the contents of this book.

Domestic Abuse Intervention Project

Dr. David Susman, PhD

EMDR Institute

Joyful Heart Foundation

Every Voice Should be Heard...

My Journey to Becoming an Advocate

Karen Hargrave

Dedication

When I thought about who I would dedicate this book to, I immediately thought of someone close to me who has been through so much since she decided to disclose her sexual abuse to me and now to her family. I thought about all of our long phone conversations, her pain, her tears, and how far she has come. Sadly, this is such a familiar scenario, and I could be describing the circumstances of dozens of women I've come to know over the past twenty-plus years. Many of them have also confided in me for long periods of time as they've disclosed abuse to their families or loved ones, or as they have struggled while healing as a survivor.

It is an all-too-familiar experience, and one far too many will relate to. I wish that weren't the case, but it is the reason I am writing this book. They are the reason I am writing it—every single one of them. Many women don't have someone they feel is safe enough to turn to with their pain, and I hope for them, maybe this book can serve that purpose until they feel safe enough to share their story with someone they trust.

But then I also thought about all the survivors I have met and known over the years and hopefully I have helped. I thought about all the things they had in common and all the things that had no similarity between them at all: things like their different walks of life, their different personalities and outlooks on life, their ages, jobs and types of work, types of lifestyle and circumstances. They have so little in common. Except for this all-too-familiar pain that so many women experience on a variety of levels, and some experience it at more than one point in their lives and at the hands of more than one perpetrator.

This book is for all of you. I see you … I believe you … I support you! I want you to know that you are not the source of the drama, the issues, or the problems in your family that your abuser caused by hurting you. He is! Go ahead and read that again. He is! Don't let anyone convince you otherwise.

Just because you have found the courage to name it and speak of it does not mean that you caused the pain or the problems that come with it. If this has happened to you or someone you care about, please seek out an advocate to help you navigate through your journey or contact your local agency that serves survivors or RAINN.org.

I hope that is what I have done with my role as an advocate and my advocacy—that it has helped people heal by bearing witness to it and being there to offer whatever I could. I hope that my being there has somehow facilitated healing for these survivors. At the very least, I hope it was clear to them that at least one person absolutely without question believed them and would be there for whatever they needed to move forward. Maybe their experience with me or another advocate could encourage them to tell others close to them about the abuse. Hopefully this could be an important step towards healing.

Details Disclaimer

This book is based on my life experience as an advocate. It is full of personal experiences, opinions, and anecdotes. It also includes some stories and examples of victims of domestic violence, sexual abuse, and sexual assault that are based on my experiences and relationships with real victims. Some names and details have been changed to protect those involved with these stories. While none of the shame associated with these crimes is theirs, they have had to deal with a wide range of issues from struggling to start a new life following these devastating crimes, protecting the anonymity of innocent family members, dealing with ignorant family members failing to believe them, protecting the wishes of those they love, and concerns of safety from abusive former spouses. The stories, examples, and testimonials are real, only names and minor details have been changed.

TRIGGER WARNING - this book contains discussions of domestic and sexual violence.

Table of Contents

Foreword

Imagine living in a world where your voice was ignored or feeling that your voice was never heard because you are considered the weak one. You never felt you could speak up for what is right. Let me introduce you to a person I'm honored to have in my life. Karen has not only been a voice for so many not strong enough to stand up for what's right, but she does so in such a way that she leaves the abuser no longer feeling "strong," but now that person is the one feeling weak and powerless.

When asked to write this foreword for Karen, I was honestly nervous. Why, you ask … well, I needed to be sure I was able to completely depict how crucial she has been in the lives of so many. For as long as I can remember, Karen has been the voice for so many people. I have had the honor of getting sneak peeks of this book, chapter by chapter, from day one. At the end of each chapter, I longed for more. This book grabs your heart and empowers you to want to become even half the caring individual Karen is.

Her path to becoming the advocate she is today is due to her confidence to always step up to help right what is wrong. As you go through this book, you are going to realize being an advocate means more than speaking for someone who is not at the point of standing their own ground. An advocate is more … and if everyone had someone like Karen in their life, I think we would all be in a place where we felt much safer to use our own voice.

Has there ever been a time where you personally needed an advocate? Unfortunately, I have; I went through something so traumatic I wasn't sure if I could make it through. Luckily for me, I do have Karen—she guided me through every hurdle and was my voice when mine was not able to work. She was the nudge I needed when I thought I was not going to be able to go further on my own. Her experience and knowledge in the area of abuse I endured were exactly what I needed. Without that, I would still be holding onto something that could very well have ended my life.

Every person deserves to be able to speak up for themselves. Unfortunately, there are situations where this is not possible. Certain people have the natural ability to speak on someone else's behalf. I truly believe being an advocate isn't taught, it comes habitually to always seeing the good in and wanting to help others. Advocates see the right, voice the right, and they won't stop until it is right. What gives some people this ability? I wish I knew.

This book you are about to read is one that is unique. It will bring you down the road of lives of people and situations where voices were silenced, but one individual paved the path for those voices to be heard. It will leave you not only wanting to read more but make you open your eyes to wanting to always stand up for what is right. To use your own voice when you see someone weaker struggling. To be the light in the life of another human. I will say it again … we all need someone like Karen in our lives!

— Isabella
Survivor

Introduction

My life as an advocate began on the worst day of my life. While I didn't know it at the time, the day my healthy forty-eight-year-old father died from complications (due to negligence) from a "routine surgery" set me on a path to a role I wouldn't fully understand for many years.

My father desperately needed a professional advocate in the hospital that week to speak up on his behalf, someone on staff who the doctors and nurses would have listened to. He was experiencing terrible post-op complications several days after surgery, when in the previous days he had been making progress towards recovery. Unfortunately, he was dead before the hospital bothered to do the test that would have easily saved his life. It was scheduled for an hour past the time when he died.

I was twenty-one and a senior in college. My whole world changed in that moment, and I would never be the same in any way. The death of my father was the most traumatic event of my life. This was not something anyone saw coming. I certainly had no idea how to cope with it, or what to do from here. I felt like I was still in shock for weeks to months after he died. After a brief time, I went back to school. I felt very guilty leaving my mom, but she wanted my sister and me to go back to school.

We tried our best to move forward, but we were figuring it out as we went along. I really don't remember very much of it. I was just going through the motions; we all were. My boyfriend and I had gotten engaged just before my dad went into the hospital for surgery, and now it felt like everything but the immediate moment in front of us was on hold.

Dad was an incredible man, and while I am sure almost everyone experiences the loss of a parent as a traumatic and life-changing event, I think that in our case, it was exceptionally painful due to the sudden preventable loss and the fact that he was such a wonderful person.

I didn't realize it at the time, and it would take decades for me to admit that anything positive could come out of this loss, but somehow, something did. It became the most dominant part of my personality as an adult … my ability to be a fierce and relentless advocate both for me and for others who could not advocate for themselves.

My focus during my graduate program was working with survivors of sexual abuse and assault, and my thesis was about using art therapy with survivors. As I moved into a professional role as a victim advocate years later, my passion for this work truly developed and my personal strengths in this area became clear. Many people may not have the life experience that has shown them the need for, or great benefits of, advocacy in nearly every situation. My professional and personal experience has highlighted these benefits in such a way that was undeniable to me, especially in working with survivors of sexual assault or abuse. This became evident to me in so many settings and different situations. One of the greatest benefits of advocacy with these individuals is the power of sharing that secret with others and beginning the process of getting rid of that shame.

Why is it so important to share your secret with others? Because there is power in breaking the silence. When you are ready, speaking out against your perpetrator can be an empowering first step in the healing process. It can help a survivor overcome shame, guilt, and fear. It can help her gain back her self-worth, confidence, and power, and it can encourage others to come forward about their sexual assault. (KMD Law)

You can become a safe person for someone else to disclose to one day. I truly hope that this book encourages you to do so. While the survivor may feel you have done so much for her just by being there for her, believing in her, and encouraging her, the benefits that it will bring to you are indescribable. I have been astounded this past year at the ways I have been impacted by helping someone so close to me walk this path towards recovering from childhood sexual abuse.

I am forever changed by knowing that she felt safe with me, and that I was one of the first people she trusted and confided in with her disclosure. It went well enough with me and my husband, and our encouragement helped her to keep going and tell more people. There were many terribly painful and difficult days, weeks, and months ahead for her. But she kept going, with a lot more people behind her, loving and supporting her. Those who didn't believe her are no longer in her (or my) life. This was huge progress and growth.

That is the goal: to move forward without those who don't believe or support you. I am grateful to her for giving me the gift of trusting me with the secret that she had been keeping her entire life. By sharing it, she was finally able to take her power back. She was creating the narrative now. It also wasn't the narrative from her past that was full of lies to support an abuser. It was just the truth. The people who didn't believe it didn't have to. She said goodbye to them for good.

I have never been prouder of anyone, and I will never be able to express that to her adequately. I had the honor of knowing that when she said, "I couldn't have come this far without you." she meant it. It was true. I had made an empirical difference for her that would last the rest of her life and change it for the better permanently. Her life today looks very different than it did a year ago. She is no longer living a lie, and that is just the beginning for her. This newfound confidence that I see in her now was never there before, but what an amazing thing it is to have witnessed it as it developed.

That is a feeling that no one can describe to you. But I encourage you to try and find out what it feels like for yourself, by helping someone in this way. I hope this book can inspire you to do so. I promise it will change your life!

Survivor Interviews, Part 1

Chapter 1
Sharing These Stories

The hardest part of writing this book for me has been the parts that I cannot put in print. Many aspects of the stories and situations that are referenced in this book are ongoing, and very raw for a lot of people very close to me. I wish that everyone in my life could feel how freeing it is to let their secrets out, but not everyone is in that place or deals with things in that way, and I have to respect the privacy of everyone involved. It isn't up to me to make that decision for others, and I admit it is something I really struggle with. For some stories, there are people who are not okay with these stories being made public, even anonymously. There are others still who were not able or willing to share their stories. It is so hard to want to share so many more aspects of these amazingly brave, strong, and resilient women's stories because I truly believe they would help others.

An important part of advocacy is meeting people where they are. And sadly, many people are not in a place where they can share or share openly. So, in many places where I wish I could put more details and specific examples, you will find general references and missing pieces instead. I have made every effort not to let this detract from the incredible examples these stories bring to the power of advocacy and how it helped in each of these instances.

For the stories on the following pages and throughout the book, I have interviewed nine survivors of sexual assault, abuse, and/or domestic violence. One survived a near-fatal knife attack from her ex-husband, who stabbed her over thirty times. Another survivor interviewed here experienced childhood sexual abuse and was unable to tell anyone until she was an adult. Another of the survivors interviewed was raped at eighteen. One woman was sexually assaulted in the military shortly after joining. You will also read about a mother and daughter who left a situation of domestic violence and how it still impacts them both to this day.

One woman was raped twice in her lifetime, decades apart. Both assaults posed the same incredible obstacles for her. Another survived insurmountable obstacles and financial burdens to free herself of the control her ex-husband was still trying to maintain over her when she found the strength to leave her abusive marriage. Many of the survivors experienced domestic or sexual violence, or unfortunately both, within their marriages.

All of these women struggled with the aftermath of abuse or violence for years. Each of them described a huge relief in no longer needing to hide any longer or live in fear. Each also expressed how this experience stays with you in ways they wished it did not. Some of them pursued the role of sexual assault/victim advocates following their personal experiences.

These women have enormous strength that most of us can only begin to imagine being required just to survive the horrible existence of daily life with an abusive partner. Most of us have never been challenged or physically and emotionally abused in the brutal ways they have been. Fortunately, most of us have not been violated in the most personal way imaginable: mind, body, and spirit.

I have asked these women to share part of their stories with us for the purpose of this book because this is not a perspective that we can easily understand. We can never truly understand if we have not been in their shoes.

Even after working in the field of sexual assault advocacy, I was surprised by how easy it was to find more than ten survivors who were willing to go on the record with their stories for my book. I don't say that because they have any reason to feel embarrassed, quite the contrary. What I mean to suggest is, again, how sad, that this is so prevalent. I found so many women who were willing to be interviewed; that I didn't even have room to include all the material that I collected.

I have asked these women some personal questions about their experience as survivors, how advocacy may or may not have helped them, whether they may have been hesitant to reach out for help, and why. I asked what kinds of things might have helped make them more comfortable telling someone what they were experiencing while it was going on—and how the first person that the survivor told made a difference to them through their reaction to what they had to say. I was curious about when and how they found the strength to go forward.

These nine women are people I admire so very much, and I know you will too after reading just a little bit about each of them here. I want to sincerely thank each of them for speaking out for themselves, and for so many others who cannot. May it bring all survivors strength as they read these incredible stories.

If this book teaches you anything, I hope it is that survivors are absolutely everywhere. They are your sisters and brothers, your mothers, your wives, your cousins, your daughters and sons, your co-workers, your friends. They are the cashier at the grocery store trying to get through the day, the waitress at your favorite restaurant, or the associate at the local clothing store. They are your neighbor, the nurse at your doctor's office, your co-worker who doesn't seem to share much about herself or to trust easily. This experience cuts evenly across all walks of life, all classes, all genders, all ages, and all identities. We all need to do better at providing a safe place for survivors to turn to when they need support.

You may never know it, because they just can't bring themselves to share it for a number of valid reasons. I would advise you to think carefully about how you present yourself to the world. Are you judgmental? Are you someone who seems approachable? Would I trust you with the biggest trauma of my life? Would I feel safe knowing that your reaction would not make me regret telling you? Would you immediately regret telling me? Or would my acceptance encourage you to tell others?

As you read these interviews, I ask you to think about the people in your life. Imagine one of them facing similar circumstances as these women (or girls at the time). What kind of characteristics would you want your loved one to be faced with if she had the courage to come forward and disclose to someone?

What type of person would she most likely feel comfortable enough with to share something so difficult and personal? What might keep her from doing so? What kind of reaction would shut her down and make her keep quiet?

What would you do if someone came to you with something this difficult? Would you know what to say? How would you handle it? Where would you turn for help and guidance? Would you have the right tools to find the information you needed to help her?

Following each interview, I have included some factual information, things you can do to make a difference in the lives of people you know, and the challenges or assumptions that survivors face.

As you read these incredible stories, I hope that you are inspired to want to help others in these ways. I truly hope that you choose to approach survivors without biases and judgment, and instead reach out to them with openness and understanding. And that you take these tips to heart as to how to be of more help to a survivor.

These incredible women, and so many with untold stories like theirs, are the reason I am writing this book. Standing by the side of one of these women this year, as she experienced the excruciating pain of disclosing childhood abuse to her entire family, has been the most profound experience of my life. Another of the women interviewed discovered so much about herself in the process of talking about it for the book. It was transformative for both of us to see the ways it impacted her as she came to understand aspects of her survivor story that she had never fully understood before, as she explained it in depth for the interview.

Even though these women and others like them knew they would likely face disbelief, judgment, and even accusations of being a liar, they somehow found the strength to come forward and disclose their secret to me and hopefully to others. And while I don't expect to be able to convey it adequately or powerfully enough to make it as meaningful for you to read about it as it was for me to experience it, I truly hope that it inspires you to want to make a difference for someone in your life.

Chapter 2
Lauren

Lauren and I first met when she became my massage therapist, over a decade ago. To describe Lauren as strong is clearly a huge understatement, as you are about to read. However, I think the most remarkable thing about her is how she has taken the challenge of these overwhelming difficulties and allowed it to be poured into her genuine, overflowing compassion for others. I am proud to call her one of my closest friends. It turns out that after all these years, when it started with her as a medical provider for me, this year we have discovered a whole other level, and the significant roles we have played in each other's lives.

Lauren's Voice

I did not know what an advocate was, prior to my experience with domestic violence. My ex-husband was using drugs at the time, which I did not know. The whole process was slow manipulation by him. It took place a little bit at a time, so that I didn't even realize it was happening. It was him pretending to be someone he wasn't, to everyone else we knew, other than me. I got a different version of him. He had convinced me that the problems in our marriage were all because of me. Our daughter, Sara, was four or five at the time.

One day when we went to the beach, his bag tipped over and some drug paraphernalia spilled out onto the beach. I quickly picked it up, grabbed it, and put it into my bag so no one in his family would see it, especially not my daughter. I acted like I had not seen the drugs so I could watch his reaction to not having them in his bag. He was clearly panicking and having withdrawal as he frantically searched for his drugs.

That is when I knew how serious it was. I started to investigate his everyday activities and to question everything I knew or believed within our relationship. It then turned the "light bulb on" as to why so many things were "not right." The fact that he constantly asked for money from me when he clearly made more than I did. The fact that he made me pay for everything and when I didn't, I was made to feel noncontributing and incompetent. The realization that when he went out at night to "take care of things at work," it was to go and get high, do drug deals, or meet another woman.

My daughter told me of the visits he and she made to a house with a woman and child (I will not name for legal reasons) where transactions were made. My daughter did not know what these transactions were, only that "Daddy was using a straw on the table with his nose." I later realized through my own investigation that this woman was a liaison to a drug cartel out of Mexico.

Without telling the details, I got his family organized to agree to an intervention for him because of his drug usage. I set up the intervention meeting, but the day before it was to happen my mother-in-law told him what was going to happen. She told him what the intentions of the meeting were. He was claiming he was not the one with the problem and that I was. She believed him.

That was when things started to escalate. It was then that I knew I was on my own. He became very threatening to me with his anger. He demanded money from me. He demanded sex from me. When I said no, he raped me and told me I "wanted it." He kept me isolated from my family who lived in another city. He portrayed me to his family and friends as someone who was "sick" and couldn't go out of the house, and that I was crazy.

When I couldn't produce any more money to give him, he came after me with his fists. On one occasion he hit his hand on the couch and tried to kick me, and when I moved, he hurt himself on the couch leg. Having done this in front of my daughter created fear for her.

This was the first time I realized it truly was not me that was the issue. I found out he was carrying a gun; his "friends" were aware of this and using drugs as well. I never told my family; I was too embarrassed and afraid. I never thought this could possibly become my life.

When I finally found the strength to tell someone, I reached out to my sister. She was very compassionate and said to call the police. They said there was nothing they could do because he hadn't done anything "yet." Was this really the standard—I had to wait for him to hurt me so they could do something to protect me?!

We had two homes at the time, so I asked him to go to the other house until we could figure things out because I had already confronted him about the drugs in addition to infidelity. He continued to use drugs, and it escalated into more serious drugs quickly. He was into cocaine, crack cocaine, and heroin. I told the police officer I talked to about what I was seeing as far as physical changes. The pupils in his eyes were tiny like a pinpoint. He told me that was a sign that he was snorting a very dangerous form of heroin, the fastest and most intense way for it to enter his system. He told me to run and take my daughter away from him as fast as I could for good, because addiction of this sort will not stop and only lead to control and domination of me and my daughter.

It took a while for me to process this, however. I filed for divorce, and he was served papers, which he would not address with me. He literally went so berserk in our living room that he did a flip in mid-air, jumping up as he lost it, and became violent. As he was losing control in his life, he was losing control over his emotions, and any sense of mastery over his actions was disappearing. Shortly after this outburst, he was cleaning his guns in our living room and made sure I watched him do that while staring at me.

A few days after that, he attempted to abscond with our daughter;- however, he could not take care of her as he never did alone. Before he left with our daughter, he placed a bullet standing straight up on the counter of our kitchen and told me he left me a gift in the kitchen. This was a clear message to intimidate me and make me fearful of him. It worked. He took the license plates off my car so I could not drive and left with my daughter in his vehicle. By the grace of God, I found them at my mother-in-law's home, and swore to God that if I was able to rescue my child, I would never look back.

I again called the police, and they told me to call the domestic violence agency as there was nothing they could do at this point. I called the domestic violence organization, and they advised me to keep calm and when he returned with my daughter to then get out and call them immediately. He had to save face with his family and came back to the marital residence with our daughter.

I needed to take her to an urgent care due to an eye infection. He would not let me take his car without "cleaning it out," and while he did that, my daughter and I escaped through another door and had a neighbor take us to an undisclosed hospital for treatment, instead of an urgent care, as I knew he would follow us. He tried.

I found later when in the shelter that he indeed went to the local urgent care to try to find us. When at the hospital, I again called the police and again called the domestic violence agency in my area and was instructed where to meet a domestic violence agency representative to have my daughter and me brought to a safe house immediately. We never were to return to the residence, as I promised to God.

I later found out that he had hired someone to kill me. One of his drug friends told me that. I called the police and was told again that there was nothing they could do. At this point, I filed for an order of protection by the advice of the domestic violence advocate. When I arrived at the first domestic violence shelter I would go to, I was shocked to see these women in long sleeves and long pants in ninety-degree weather, to cover their numerous bruises and scars.

I felt I did not belong there. I did not have any marks on me. I was not like these women but the advocate at the shelter told me that my marks and scars were just as damaging, and I should be the first to walk in that door. Just because they could not be seen did not make them less real.

The criminal justice system and the legal system were set up to support him, not me. I had to prove he was doing criminal acts by dealing and using drugs. I had to prove he was a psychopathic narcissist by having the test done myself. I had to prove that he was using drugs to the extent of abuse by flying in the scientist who performed the tests for me to validate for the court that he was indeed addicted. I had to prove he was lying. I had to prove everything I was doing was in the interest of protecting my daughter and myself. The court system allowed him to go through six attorneys before my attorney demanded a reason for the previous attorneys dropping him as a client. The attorney before his last one admitted he could not represent a client who continued to lie.

It was only when I was in the protective surroundings of the domestic violence advocates that I felt safe enough to proceed. The system protects the abuser more than it protects the victim. It is set up for the victim to prove how bad the abuse is. It took me nearly a decade to get away from him and bankrupted me in the process. Everything I had worked for monetarily was gone. I had to start over from ground zero.

When talking to the group at the shelter, the advocate made it clear the role she played. She was there to help us see what we were too close to our situations to see. It was at this meeting that I first saw the power-and-control wheel. This is a tool created by a domestic violence program to explain abusive behavior. You will see it in Chapter 23 and in the Appendix.

For me, seeing it on paper made such a difference. It wasn't me wondering who was causing all these problems any longer or doubting myself as the cause. It was someone else showing me what his behavior was in black and white. It was on paper, and somehow that made it real. It showed me that this really was him and his problem.

What I got from an advocate was encouragement, support, information, and help. I was told that I was the exception, not the rule, in that I left the first time I knew how bad it was, and I never went back. I learned that most women go back many times (seven or eight) before they can make the break and leave for good. Although I was going through my own pain, I wanted to help the women in the shelter to not go back.

At one time at the shelter, one of the other residents was on the phone speaking to her abuser. She gave him the phone number at the shelter, which was against the rules. When she got off the phone, I told her that she could not do that. She told me that he would not come here: "He said he loves me, and he misses me." While she was talking to him, I wrote on a piece of paper:

I love you = I want to control you.
I want you home = I want to imprison you.
I miss you = I want to rape you.
I miss my son = he is the pawn.

I hung this note by the phone. It still hangs there today as far I know.

When I relocated to the area where my family was from, I had to attend domestic violence groups there. He again tried to abscond with Sara while she was in school. He violated the order of protection and came to my house high and intoxicated and scared both my daughter and me, trying to break the front door in. The police eventually arrested him, and he was sent to jail. When the police brought him to court, he was handcuffed, heavily guarded and shackled, and still I was visibly shaking while having to face him.

That again is where the role of the advocate came into play. She was there to come to court with me and helped me get through it. She had to speak to the judge for me when I could not speak to him. She literally held me upright through the court proceedings. I just kept thinking of the "friends" he had and what he could have them do to me or my daughter. This advocate was so helpful, so reassuring, so kind, and so strong. I couldn't have been there without her. Thank you, Anne.

When in a situation of abuse, most times victims believe they are the cause of the problem. They have been so manipulated over time that sometimes an advocate needs to show them that the abuser is the culprit. Advocates show victims of abuse the examples of why the abuser is the perpetrator. When victims are being abused, basic instincts and survival skills kick in, and they learn to live moment to moment, not day to day. There is a difference. Living moment to moment is all you can do to survive. They are on high alert, constantly aware of the possible next threat. Everything is a potential source of danger. This literally never goes away; it becomes a chronic situation of living in fear.

I later learned that the amygdala of your brain enlarges when you are in danger. This is the part of the brain that controls your fight or flight response to fear and danger. For people who are chronically in danger, such as soldiers, people in war zones, or trauma victims, the amygdala never goes back to its original size even after the threats are gone. When you have lived in fear so long that the only thing you can do is live moment to moment, this is part of the reason why. It is your brain chemistry. That is why anyone suffering from Post-Traumatic Stress Disorder (PTSD) only navigates through life and doesn't "adjust" to life.

Other obstacles that got in my way of getting help included being conditioned in society throughout my working career as a woman. I always had to work twice as hard to be accepted half as much. I was brought up in a man's world where women are inferior to men. I worked very hard to be viewed differently by the men I worked with. I wanted to be respected as much as my male colleagues were. It was difficult to be successful and not looked upon as being an equal.

I felt that way in my marriage and tried very much to be accepted, and in the process was manipulated, deceived, and hurt deeply. When it escalated to abuse and violence, there was nothing the police could do for me until he did something physical to me. There is nothing that I know of that the police can do for emotional and mental abuse. Where could I go from there? There were similar issues with the court system. I needed more evidence that he was violent to act against him and keep him from my daughter. I did not want my daughter to see her father treat her mother this way, and in the future, allow her partners to treat her the same way.

The advocates at the domestic violence shelter were the only ones who explained all aspects of abuse. Mental, emotional, spiritual, physical, and financial abuse. The advocate can help to deprogram you from the years of brainwashing you have endured. Abusers are excellent at isolating you from others who would support you and question their behavior of encouragement to belittle the situation.

Advocates are patient and steady, as they say the things you need to hear, as you are ready to hear them. At this point, you really can't process anything else but these small bits of information at a time. Therefore, the advocates may repeat these proclamations of knowledgeable proficiencies over and over. Just so that we can process on our time.

This is why the role of the advocate is so important, and for so many other reasons as well. The advocate is there for support to help you get through that moment-to-moment existence, until you can do so on your own. When it is your crisis, you are too close to it to see it. The advocate can pull you away from it just enough to show you the examples of what is happening to you, because perspective can be askew due to the inability to pull oneself away from the situation. You need distance to see it. It is like a three-dimensional picture that you put close to your face, and the farther you take it away from your face, the picture actually comes into focus. One must step out and away from the abusive conditioning to see the full picture.

In addition, an advocate can also help the children of adult victims by placing them with their own counselors and advocates. I was so grateful for that for my daughter. She benefited from speaking with a neutral party who was loving, understanding, compassionate, and insightful. Often, we do not realize the effect the abuse is having on the children during our own abuse. We think we protect our children or that they will not remember because they are young; however, their scars can be deeper than ours. The advocates recognize this when we don't or can't because we are too focused on dealing with our own abuse and thinking we are protecting our children.

Without that support of the advocate in my life, I have no doubt that I would be dead now, due to the fact of his hiring someone to kill me. I could not think clearly enough, because of living in a moment-to-moment situation trying to survive and protect my daughter from harm. The advocate kept me safe, calm, and directed me on how to properly navigate the legal system while supporting me in the chaotic court system.

While every situation is different, there are some key things that everyone can do to offer help in a situation. First of all, listen. Just listen, and don't try to shove it under the rug. It will not go away, no matter how uncomfortable it makes you. Do not tell someone, "You must be mistaken; he isn't like that." You have no idea how he treated me or my child. You see his public persona, not how he is to us in private.

Someone in this situation is so embarrassed that their spouse has been treating them in such a terrible way. They don't need other people judging them for being in this situation. Other people only see the person that he wants them to see. There is a lot of self-talk with things like, "People would not want to believe me if I did have the courage to come forward. This is not the person that I knew. How could I be in this situation or let it get this bad?"

The fear of not being believed is so strong, and you are again targeted as the one who can't be believed. That starts a cycle of not knowing who you can trust. You don't know who is safe, so you just don't tell anyone. In some ways, the more people you tell, the more they don't believe you. I felt embarrassed, and disappointed in myself. We have expectations of ourselves, and I felt like I had failed. I couldn't admit it to myself, much less anyone else. It was about expectations. People looked at me as a strong person. If they knew I was being abused and I stayed in the situation, they would see me as weak and know that I had failed.

It wasn't until many years later that I saw myself as a strong woman. The fear was finally gone. I slowly developed the confidence to do anything. I was stronger than I had ever been before. Even though that fear was gone, I never stopped looking over my shoulder. I felt like "there were others like him." And he still had his "friends." To give you an idea of how long this went on, for over five years, there was a car parked down my street to do surveillance on me and my daughter. My ex-husband passed away in 2009 from his own actions, and to this day I still find myself looking, watching, wondering if someone is watching me.

I knew there were so many other women like me. I didn't want to be skeptical of people as I have always been a trusting person. I believed if I were a good person and treated people well that I would be treated in kind. The advocates showed me that the world is not quite as I had believed. They showed me that I had developed the tools to recognize manipulators, abusers, and deceitful people. Those are skills I have used my whole life. For those advocates, I am eternally grateful.

If there was anything I could tell others, it would be that you never know what someone is going through, so be kind, and listen. An example of this is the case of a woman from the city where I live. A loving wife and mother who was brutally beaten by her husband with a baseball bat (she had an order of protection against him), and although she was in the hospital recovering, he snuck into the hospital as a janitor and poisoned her with cyanide and killed her. His family thought he "was a good guy."

While you may know a few details about a situation, you are only seeing what others are allowing you to see. You don't know the whole story. And while it is difficult not to judge, try. Try very hard. You have no idea what that person has been through, what they've endured or how that abuser has tormented them for years, decades. That is something you can't understand unless you have been through it.

I was afraid to come forward to certain people. My Catholic upbringing made me susceptible to that old Catholic guilt about divorce, what a family was supposed to be, etc. Again, a lot of it comes down to expectations and what others think. When I finally did come forward, I had all the support in the world from my immediate family. However, at the same time, when I finally had the courage to talk about it, many gave me the indication they didn't want to hear it or couldn't hear it. They didn't want their version of that person to be shattered and changed forever.

Although I have only given you a glimpse of the details of the entirety of what happened over a fifteen-year period, the most important aspect of this is how my daughter and I survived through advocacy. It has been over twenty-five years, and the thoughts and effects of this never ever go away. I am still triggered by certain experiences today, and I still react as does my daughter. It has been a continual process of recovering from this trauma. I still work with advocates, and Karen Hargrave has been an important advocate who is a cornerstone in the continuation of advocacy support in my life. Advocates are truly amazing people who genuinely care about supporting and fighting for the victims and survivors. They are our voices. They are our gift, and I am forever grateful.

Chapter 3
Common Survivor Mental Health Disorders

Survivors may have to deal with numerous mental health issues. Below is a list of common disorders (from *KMDLaw.com*).

- Thoughts of suicide or attempted suicide

- Self-harm, cutting, scratching, pulling out hair

- Overwhelming feelings of sadness, hopelessness, unhappiness

- Fixating on past failures/self-blame

- Sleeping too much/not getting enough sleep

- Having intrusive thoughts about the event

- Easily startled

- Constantly feeling worried or scared

- Feeling anxious most of the time

- Uncontrolled overthinking

- Severe lack of energy

Chapter 4
The Impact Lauren Had on Me

Including Lauren's survivor story in my book has been very personal to me because she has impacted my life in such a significant way. When I first met her, I was struck not only by her genuine empathy and caring, but also by her intuitive nature. It was obvious that Lauren had a very special gift of sensing and knowing what your body needed.

A serious car accident in 2000 had left me with injuries and suffering that seemed impossible to heal or alleviate. It was eleven years after the accident that I found Lauren and her amazing abilities for healing. When recently looking up the date I began seeing her (for this book), I was stunned to realize that it had been so long. I was honestly shocked that I had not given up by then, because of the constant pain and frustration, both physical and emotional.

Looking back at it, I was surprised I had been able to continue to search for something that would help me feel better. Quite honestly, it was completely exhausting to be in pain and experience constant disappointment, and to pay a lot of money in the process. Remembering that absolutely nothing had worked so far, even I was impressed that I had kept going. This is where a trait I have possessed my whole life would come in handy—I am *stubborn!*

But even after so many attempts and disappointments with so many practitioners, there was something about Lauren that was different, and I knew it from that first day. I do believe that the simple fact of knowing her, and seeing her every month, had an enormous impact on me and my own skills as an advocate.

I thought I had already done a pretty good job of being my own medical advocate, but Lauren showed me an example of how to continue to do so and demand the very best care for my body. She also had such confidence and grace that she didn't need to overstate it. She just revealed it over and over again in the way she tried different approaches and did so with such great compassion that this was far more than just her job. It was her calling. Over the many years that she has worked on my body, we became friends, and she eventually became a very close confidant.

During some extremely difficult times, I leaned on her a lot. Whenever I had something physically bothering me that I could not figure out, even long after I had moved out of state, she continued to be the person I would reach out to ask for help and guidance. No matter how busy she was, and how long a day she had already had, I would always hear from her, and she would give me her very best attention and effort. Just like when she was seeing me in person, she was always right.

She knew what was wrong and how to treat it. She would take the time to describe what to do, how to fix it. Sometimes we would even Facetime so she could show me a technique I could use on myself or have my husband use. It has been six years since we moved out of the state where I first met Lauren, and she continues to be my consultant for everything medical, and a lot of things emotional as well.

She is my mentor in a lot of ways. I aspire to be as knowledgeable, smart, intuitive, and giving as she is. She is a great role model for any human being who cares about others. She taught me how to be a better advocate without even trying, or knowing she was doing it. I didn't even truly realize it until I began to organize my thoughts for this book. She inspires me to be better at everything.

Lauren disclosed to me fairly early on in our relationship that she was a survivor of domestic violence. I felt honored that she had trusted me with this information, and it was such an important part of her history. It impacted every part of her life. I never wanted to do a disservice to it by failing to realize that hearing me talk about my work as an advocate in this field (in a general way) could be a trigger for her. That doesn't even begin to discuss the number of issues I would bring to her personally years later, long after I had left that job and the role professionally, that I would confide in her about. This could have very easily triggered her and been far too much for a survivor to handle, but not for Lauren.

There is one night I remember when I called her about a family member in significant crisis, and I sensed that it was triggering her to talk about it. We were both crying on the phone together, and I asked her to let me turn to someone else with it. She said no—that she was okay, and we continued to cry and talk. That night in particular she was an enormous help to me in a way that very few people could have been. She had an understanding of abuse that someone who hasn't been through it themselves would not have. She knew in that moment that is exactly what I needed: someone who could truly understand, listen, and help me get through it myself while I helped the person close to me who was going through it.

Seeing what Lauren and her relationship with me did for me, to encourage me through her advocacy with my medical condition, allowed me to see what advocacy could truly do for someone else when used correctly and effectively. The inspiration, encouragement, and hope for the future that I finally felt about my medical condition were making me understand the implications of being a sexual assault victim advocate, and what those implications could mean to the survivors I would work with, if I did my role half as well as Lauren fulfilled hers.

It gave me a new motivation and knowledge to build on, something to strive for: to always do better, to always do more for that person, to always fight for what was right, even when it was unpopular, when the odds of making progress were against you, and when it was not easy to do. That is something I have struggled with my entire life, and for the first time, I think I had accepted that this had to be based on how I felt about it—me alone. I couldn't take too much influence from outside sources to heart and allow it to get in the way of me pursuing what I now began to feel was a calling. I couldn't stop doing something I was so dedicated to because sometimes it wasn't going to be easy or well received.

I started to look at things through a different lens. Instead of worrying about "How is this going to go over?" "What would people think or say?" —it became, "Is this the right thing to do?" "Will this person's life be changed for the better if we do this?"

I was pursuing this role in a more significant way than ever, and that had a lot to do with the impact that knowing Lauren was having on me. I could feel that I had become a better advocate just from taking in what I felt when working with her. I will be forever grateful to Lauren for helping me manage my pain and become physically better than I had been before seeing her. I still struggle with my physical pain and symptoms, but I am much better than before I went to her. But almost equal to her contribution to my physical health is what I have gained from knowing her personally. She inspires me to be a better, more empathetic, caring advocate.

Chapter 5
Katie

I first met Katie fairly soon after she was brutally attacked. Years later, we would reconnect over a protest movement at the agency where I had worked. She did a lot of public speaking, and her story of survival was inspirational to all who heard it. She graciously agreed to allow me to interview her and share her story in my book. I can't thank her enough for sharing it. She has come back after being so viciously assaulted, and still manages to see the good in people. She continues to help others in whatever ways she can. I so admire her for that.

Katie's Voice

Can you tell me a little bit about the life circumstances that caused you to seek out the help of a domestic violence/sexual assault (DV/SA) advocate (*if you did*)?

I had kicked my husband out after being married more than twenty years. He had been abusive to me our whole marriage, and now he was harassing me in ways small enough that the police couldn't (or wouldn't) do anything about it. One day when I didn't know what else to do, I went to a local agency for victims of domestic abuse. I just sat in a room for a while, and someone brought me a drink and gave me peace and time to think. I slowly began talking to someone there about what was happening with my husband.

Soon after that time, one night my husband came into my home and stabbed me over thirty times. When he finally stopped, he went to leave the house and he passed my daughter in the hallway, and she asked him what he was doing there. He replied, "I just killed your mother, you might want to call the cops."

As I drifted in and out of consciousness, I heard the police asking my daughter who did it. She answered, "My father did it."

In what ways did having an advocate make a difference in your situation?

It wasn't until I was in the hospital that I had an advocate assigned to me. It gave me direction, and she showed me what steps to take. It was empowering for me to know what steps to take. My advocate never told me what to do. She always said, "It is up to you," or "These are your choices." I felt like someone had my back. She listened to me, and she visited me every day as I recovered.

What things would you not have known to do on your own without the help of an advocate?

I would have had no direction; I didn't know any of the steps of the legal process. I was on painkillers at the time and also had several surgeries. I didn't know the legal system. I never realized I had a say in him not taking the plea bargain he was offered. If I had been aware of it, I would have objected to him taking it. I wish I had known more about the law. Without my advocate, I would have known even less.

Try to describe the difference it makes to have someone advocating or being there for you.

She would encourage me to talk to a therapist when I needed to. She did not make me go, but she would encourage me to, as well as to go to other support groups and art therapy. She helped me to find services that I would not have known about.

She reminded me that the shame was not mine. This came up when it was ninety-five degrees, and I was wearing turtlenecks in August to hide my scars. She came to my home one day and told me to go back into the house and change. I had nothing to hide or be ashamed of. At that point, I needed someone to tell me that.

What difference does that support make in a situation like yours?

Everyone who spoke to me at the agency I was receiving services from made me feel stronger. They offered me several opportunities to share my story, to help others. Every choice was up to me. I was empowered to decide what was best for me.

Do you ever think about how your life might be different if you hadn't had that support?

Yes, I do. I would probably be a recluse and stay hidden alone at home. There are still a lot of things I do because I am scared, like putting cans by the door so I will hear it if someone comes in. Those habits come back to me more when times get harder—like now, as I anticipate him getting out of prison soon.

What advice would you give to someone who had a family member or close friend come forward to disclose their abuse or assault to you?

I would encourage them to say, "These are your choices," "It is your decision," and other things I heard from my advocate. I know myself how hard it is to say those things instead of "Run!"—which is my instinct.

I learned from my advocate that it takes someone more than six or seven times before they leave an abusive partner for good. If I am trying to help someone with their abusive situation, I tell them that I will always be there for them, even if they choose not to leave.

What difference does that first person's reaction make—positive? negative?

The agency where I went was so supportive. I knew I had a safe place I could count on because of their reaction when I told them my story. Being with people who supported and believed me meant everything. I knew after my attack that I could go there and trust anyone who worked there.

What were some obstacles that kept you from reaching out for help sooner?

My mother being dismissive. Me being embarrassed. I really didn't want anyone to know. I was unaware of the help that was available for domestic violence. Money was a big obstacle.

He threatened to kill my children. He stood by their bedroom door with a shotgun saying, "If you walk out, I will kill them both." He threatened he would kill my dad.

Did you ever feel shame or embarrassment about your situation? And if so, why do you think that is, since you had done nothing wrong?

Yes. I know now it wasn't my fault, but I was ashamed then.

Were there specific people in your life you couldn't or wouldn't tell? Why?

My mother was dismissive, and I was embarrassed. There are still certain things I can't talk about. I could not tell my grandmother—because she was strong and she knew I should leave him, and she told me so. I could not let her see me as weak.

What was it about their reaction that you feared?

I was afraid for my grandmother to see me in that situation. I didn't want her to see me experience that.

How is your life different now from when you were in an abusive relationship, or once you began to heal from your abuse/assault?

I make my own rules. My bills are paid. I do what I want to do. I got to see my child have children and can enjoy them without fear. I don't live in fear anymore.

What are the major differences?

I no longer live in fear of every reaction.

What else would you want someone reading this book to know?

Be supportive of someone who reaches out to you, no matter what. Make sure that they know that your support is not conditional on them leaving the abusive relationship. Don't tell them to just "run"—it is not that simple.

Did you ever feel judged or unsafe to tell people close to you?

Yes.

What did they say or do specifically to make you feel this way?

It was nothing specific, it was me feeling scared in general.

What could they have done better that would have made a difference to you?

I believe that some people knew about the abuse and didn't say anything. Truthfully, I think at some point, I would have dismissed anyone who said something about it. I didn't talk about it with anyone. I had to be ready.

Chapter 6
The Power in Breaking the Silence

An article on *KMDLaw.com* makes this fact clear: "When you are ready, speaking out against your perpetrator can be an empowering first step in the healing process."

The article lists the following positive effects of speaking up:

- Overcome shame, guilt and fear.

- Begin the healing process.

- Feel relief that your perpetrator is being held accountable.

- Gain back your self-worth, confidence and power.

- Help others to come forward about their sexual assault.

- Re-establish better personal relationships.

Chapter 7
Lynn and Devynn

Lynn and I first met when we were both moving from and to the same cities. We had a family connection through my work, and we immediately hit it off. Since we now live in the same neighborhood, I have gotten to know her whole family. It is no surprise that she has the strength and belief in herself that she does. Without doubt, this was what gave her the confidence to leave her abusive situation as quickly as she did. I am honored to know her and call her my friend.

Lynn's Voice

My first husband physically assaulted me in our home. Days later I filed a restraining order, and when I went to court, there was a representative from the local domestic violence agency there who I met and spoke to. I listened to what she had to say, and what my options were. I never contacted them after that.

Looking back at it, I think I should have gotten in touch with the domestic violence agency again and asked for counseling for me and my daughter, Devynn. I should have asked what my rights were as far as leaving with her and trying to get a new place. (He threatened to take custody if I went into an apartment complex where there was a known registered offender, not that I knew that at the time.) So having someone by my side to help voice my safety concerns and mental well-being, I think it would have helped me deal with later relationships down the line.

If I had the support of an advocate, I probably wouldn't have been intimidated by him, and would know the legalities, or avenues, that could have helped me get out on my own with my child. I would advise others in this situation to see a professional counselor through the whole ordeal. It may make a huge difference in how you feel about yourself, and how you view other relationships.

It makes a positive impact to tell people, based on the fact that it's out in the open. It happened, and I'm coping with the aftermath. I don't have to shield or conceal the incident anymore. As far as obstacles that got in the way of me reaching out for help sooner, I was afraid to ask for help, out of fear that he would retaliate. I feared that he would do more harm and take our child. I was afraid of what people would think or say. Too much fear was instilled, so that took over my voice to speak up.

Yes, I mostly certainly did feel shame and embarrassment. I didn't think my marriage would go down that road. I was very young when I got married and wanted a "happily ever after." I did not have a fraction of happiness at all from the get-go. Yet I pretended my life was fine, up until the night of the assault. Then I felt shame because I let myself stay for so long. It took one night of abuse to open my eyes completely and tell myself, "This is not my life."

It was hard for me to tell certain people in my life at first. I didn't tell my grandmother at first, although she knew deep down that I wasn't happy at all. I actually didn't tell a lot of family about the abuse until years later. I just didn't want to hear them say they knew he wasn't a good person from the beginning. I wanted to shield them from that, because we didn't have any abuse in our family. I knew my grandmother felt my pain in her soul. I didn't want anyone to hurt like I did or feel like they had to do or say anything to try to make it better, when the damage was already done.

My life has changed significantly since. I got my "girl power" back. I stood up for myself in relationships after that marriage. I ended things that weren't making me happy. I stopped a relationship from taking over my life, and said it just wasn't enough.

I have since remarried, and I have a husband who treats me like I have always wished for, as a partner. He loves me for me and doesn't ask me to alter myself in any way. My ex-husband was a heavy drinker, very controlling. My husband now doesn't have a drinking problem, doesn't control me, encourages me to do things that make me happy, and supports anything I want to pursue. I have stability, no fear, no nervousness, no being on guard 24/7. It's called peace—I found that.

I would want others reading this book to know that it will be hard if you are in this situation, but one day at a time, the pieces of you that feel shattered will be put back together. And one day you will look back on all of this and feel so damn proud of the person you became and what you fought for, and who you fought for—yourself.

Before I told people about the abuse, I felt ashamed, like waiting for someone to say, "I told you so." After it came out, I felt relieved actually. I did not feel judged in any way; they felt bad for me. They had a feeling he was not a good person, but we avoided talking about him. Honestly, I had a great support system for the initial leaving and getting out of the house. I don't think there was anything they could have done differently. I had to make some tough decisions, but they supported me in that.

I interviewed Lynn's daughter, as I am fortunate enough to know them both personally. I was interested to learn that Devynn did not know about the domestic violence her mother experienced until she was quite a bit older. Lynn's situation was unique in that she left at the first instance of domestic violence, and never went back. Lynn was able to keep it from Devynn until she was old enough to be told the truth. It was not until Devynn was in college that she became interested in advocacy. She attended the University of Tampa as a psychology and criminology major, and an agency, The Spring of Tampa Bay, came to her school and did a presentation on their agency and the advocacy they provide to domestic violence survivors. It was at this time that she became interested in learning more about working in a role that focused specifically on helping survivors of domestic violence. Next year, she will be pursuing a dual master's degree in forensic and legal psychology, as well as clinical mental health counseling. She hopes to pursue advocacy at the federal level. Below you will find some of the highlights from my conversation with her. Thank you to both Lynn and Devynn for sharing your stories.

Devynn's Voice

I was very grateful that I had been unaware of my mom's experience with domestic violence with my father until I was old enough to understand it. I was glad that I had not witnessed it or had any memory of it. I currently work at a domestic violence shelter in Tampa. Because of my personal experience with Mom leaving her situation the first time it happened, it was confusing to me at first when the survivors at the shelter were frequently going back to their abuser multiple times before they left for good (if they did leave).

My experience at the shelter truly taught me about the cycle of abuse, that the relationship may not always seem "bad," and that in between the incidents, the abuser may apologize and promise to change. I now understand that it is part of a cycle that causes many of the survivors to return home until they too recognize that domestic violence is often a continuous cycle.

When someone is in this situation, what they want is for someone to just listen without judging or giving advice. They don't need to be judged or told what to do, or how to solve their problems. You shouldn't try to solve it for them, say "I told you so," or bash the abuser. Survivors face many biases and judgments from friends and family members.

When speaking to people who don't have the training that I have, one of the most common things I hear is "Why didn't she just leave?" Even if leaving was that easy, which of course it is not, leaving does not cause the abuse to magically end. In fact, leaving is the most dangerous time for a woman in an abusive relationship. The chance of her being physically harmed rises dramatically when she leaves, removing the control the abuser has had over her.

Chapter 8
What Advocacy Means

Advocacy: Any action that speaks in favor of, recommends, argues for a cause, supports or defends, or pleads on the behalf of others.

The meaning of advocacy is to bring change, whether through public awareness, offering support, contracting advocacy services, or influencing policies for a particular issue. Advocacy helps people to express their views, thoughts, and concerns.

There are three types of advocacies:

- Self-advocacy

- Individual advocacy

- Systems advocacy

So why do I feel so strongly about advocacy? Hopefully my introductory chapter gave you a good idea of how and why advocacy became so important to me. I really never realized it was developing as a passion of mine, until so many years later. But I guess I became so passionate about advocacy and in particular, in relation to survivors of sexual assault, after the year and a half I spent in the clinical program where all of the children had been survivors of sexual abuse.

I was also only beginning to understand the impact that being sexually abused would have on these children for the rest of their lives, no matter what kind or how much therapy they had. The numerous personal incidents that had happened to me during the time I was in that program also contributed to that passion and my determination to make a difference. The work I had done on my thesis also reinforced how useful art therapy was for these survivors.

In my lifetime, I have utilized advocacy in the following ways and for the following people:

- Survivors of sexual assault, domestic violence, or abuse

- Advocating for myself and others to acquire needed medical care, diagnosis, and treatment

- In the school system for both my children to make sure all their needs were being met

- For friends and family in dozens of situations when they were struggling with a difficult problem, and needed the cooperation of a system to acquire the appropriate services (medical, educational, counseling, chemical dependency, alcohol dependency, legal, eating disorders, and so much more)

So, what are the basics of advocacy, and what skills are most essential?

- Communication skills

- Empathy, but not so empathetic that you get too attached or so involved with the person or their problem that you lose objectivity and the ability to be effective

- Organization

- Time management

- Active and reflective listening

- Taking action one step at a time

- Assertiveness and an expectation to have your needs met

- Researching how to best solve problems

- Creative approaches to find solutions

- Willing to negotiate, defend, even fight for what is right or deserved in the situation or environment

- Not being afraid of being disliked or unpopular, unconcerned about being considered abrasive or being labeled as bitchy or demanding

II.
The Job I Did Very Well and How It Followed Me for Years

Chapter 9
My Role as An Advocate for Victims of Sexual Assault

Note: For the purposes of this chapter (and beyond) I will use the word victim to refer to the victim of a *recent* assault. If we are responding to the hospital, that person has just experienced a crime and is therefore a "victim." I completely acknowledge and respect that most survivors of sexual abuse and assault prefer the term survivor, once that assault or abuse is in the *past*. You will notice that distinction throughout this book. I will also refer to the victims as "her" or "she" as this is most often the case. However, we know that sexual assault can happen to anyone regardless of gender or gender identity.

Once I felt I was ready to go back to working outside the home, I wasn't entirely sure of what I wanted to do. I talked about it a lot with a friend, and at one point, she asked me if I would speak to her friend, who had just been assaulted in a grocery store parking lot and beaten up in the middle of the day. It seemed to be an attempt to abduct her. Knowing about my counseling experience, my friend asked if this woman could call me. I said, "Of course."

We talked, and as she went through the details of the attack and her feelings about the attack and the time since it had happened, I could almost feel her getting lighter and more relaxed as we spoke. Maybe this was the direction I needed to follow, to get back into a counseling role in a part-time capacity.

I saw an ad for the local Rape Crisis Center. They were seeking volunteers to respond for victims at area hospitals. Maybe this would be something I could excel at doing. So I called and scheduled an interview with the coordinator of the sexual assault volunteers. I wondered, what did that term mean exactly?

It meant that when a recent victim of sexual assault or abuse arrived at the hospital for medical treatment or an exam at one of our county hospitals, the volunteer on call would respond and be there for support, questions, paperwork for funding, and yes, most of all—advocacy. I was in.

I liked the idea of being there for someone who needed me, someone who maybe didn't have anyone else. It occurred to me that being there for someone at the worst moment of their life could be an amazing thing to do. I had dealt with sexual assault extensively when I worked briefly as a therapist but had never done this type of crisis response work. I was intimidated by all that I didn't know and would need to learn.

So I signed up to attend the training, and I learned about all the things I needed to know regarding the various systems someone would need to navigate through: the legal system, criminal justice system, medical system, and so on. I learned about the resources that were available to someone immediately following a sexual assault. I learned what options a victim has: whether to get medical care, sexually transmitted infection prevention, pregnancy prevention, HIV prophylaxis, future screenings for diseases for the next several months, etc.

We learned facts about the laws, medical information, and legal processes. We learned how to fill out the paperwork through the state that allowed victims to receive compensation for expenses related to the crime. For example, if they had medical bills, if they had to move so their perpetrator could not find them, prescription costs, and other costs. We also did hours of role-plays of real scenarios that volunteers had responded to in past calls. It would prepare us for the various scenarios, circumstances, and challenges.

Perhaps one of the biggest things it did was to prepare us for how not to fill the silence because we were uncomfortable with it. How to just be there for someone in the moment, and not have to talk because it was uncomfortable to have it be quiet. We learned to always take the lead from the victim. It isn't about what we need to say or do—what he or she needs is what should dictate what is happening or being said.

We practiced not asking questions. We were not interviewing victims; we didn't need all the facts. The police would do that if they were called, and we did not want to make them go through that more than once. It was always up to the victim whether the police were called, unless a weapon was used in the attack. Anytime a gun was used, the police were called automatically, according to state law.

Chapter 10
Some of What a Victim Experiences

I also learned the challenges a victim of assault faces. Although many of these were obvious without having this role, some were not. I watched as the burden was clearly placed on the victim each and every time: to find and seek help, to get medical care when she had no means to get there or pay for it, to put the pieces of her life back together, to face the police and convince them that she was telling the truth about an experience so humiliating she could barely speak. In many instances, victims were asked for proof or evidence that this was not a consensual sexual experience.

There were many things I was now exposed to that were so disturbing—not the least of which was that many of the victims I would see at the hospitals were not outraged by what had just happened to them. Many were not even surprised. Sadly, it seemed that their life experience may have taught them that they didn't deserve any better than this experience or that it was a "normal" part of life.

As many people know, if someone is sexually abused as a child, they are far more likely to be a victim again in their lifetime. This revictimization is not completely understood, but the statistics prove that it is real. One study purports that being sexually assaulted once means that a woman is thirty-five times more likely than others to be revictimized. The percentage of women who were raped as children or adolescents and raped as adults was more than twice the percentage among women without an early rape history.

The most frequently accepted statistic on the percentage of women who will be sexually abused or assaulted in their lifetime is one in three. It is obviously likely to be much higher, as the accepted statistic on how many women report such abuse is one in ten. And of course, if you broaden that definition to include harassment, stalking, and inappropriate comments, expectations, or treatment in the workplace, it goes up even higher. I would venture to guess that most of us know multiple women who have been directly impacted by at least one of these forms of abuse.

Two questions:

1. Why is this so pervasive? Other than the obvious fact: the patriarchal structure of our society that much of the world seems just fine accepting.

2. Why don't people (both men and women) care more, to the point that they actively do something about it?

Both questions have been plaguing me for decades and are probably what kept me doing this work for so long, even when it became increasingly difficult for me personally. So why am I so much more outraged than most people about this issue? Why am I made to feel like this is a flaw with *me*?

My answer to the question of why I am so outraged, is usually "Why *aren't* you?" "Are you really okay with a woman being raped, harassed, abused, or assaulted?" I don't think my outrage should be put into question, but rather your indifference to this issue should be. I got over being labeled "difficult," "argumentative," and "humorless" a long time ago. And for the record, people who have hatred or hostility towards feminists in general often label us as humorless.

What that really means is that we are humorless about being mistreated, abused, raped, paid less for the same work, objectified, treated like we are dumb just because we are women, made to feel like our opinions don't matter, and so on. Yes, of that I am guilty. Anyone who knows me knows that I am far from humorless, about anything that is actually funny. I just don't find abuse and rape funny. But trust me, when one of those misogynistic men who holds those beliefs about women like me finds out that their daughter has been sexually assaulted, there is no one he would rather have in that hospital room advocating for her than me.

I've met many such men over the years, and it is amazing how outraged they become when the sexism of the world is now claiming their daughter as a target. Suddenly the tables are turned, and maybe they see just a tiny bit of what happens when misogyny is allowed to run rampant and those beliefs about women being objects are made acceptable. When those patterns translate into someone they love being hurt, things quickly look different to them.

Chapter 11
Learning My New Role

Once I had completed the classroom portion of the training for my new role, it was time to go on real calls with a mentor volunteer. What should I expect? What was this really going to be like? The mentor volunteers and supervisor of the program assured us that we were ready, but I wasn't sure. When I finally got my first call, nothing could have prepared me. It felt like I was invading this amazingly intimate and private moment in a hospital exam room with a total stranger.

It takes a significant amount of time to mentally understand and truly accept that this crime was really not about sex, but about power and control. Of course, we learn that first thing in our classroom training, but once you start seeing real examples of it right in front of you, you realize that sex is just the weapon used to exert power and control. It is about degradation and humiliation. And as one of my eloquent friends and co-workers used to say, "It is about one person saying to another, my needs are more important than anyone else's."

Also, my early experiences at the hospital as an advocate were with both female and male victims. This was not at all what I had expected. Maybe it was just a reminder to me that anyone can be a victim, which I already knew. It was also a good reminder that rape is about power and control. Those calls with male victims were a bit awkward and difficult. I was in the room when the victims were having the physical exam and evidence collected, and all that goes along with that. I wasn't sure I was going to be able to do it. Soon it became clear that even with the unexpected change in circumstances of the victims being male, and some other events that were particularly difficult about these calls, I actually was doing the work. I was getting comfortable and gaining confidence and competence with each call. I quickly realized that it was even more of a challenge to make a male victim comfortable at the ER.

I soon discovered that most male victims would not want a male advocate to be there with them. All victims experience shame, even though the shame should never belong to the victim, but our society sends us quite a different message. The message to men could not be clearer. Vulnerability equals weakness. Many men do not accept that rape is not about sex, but about power and control. For most men, the thought of being raped by another man would, at the very least, question their masculinity. Imagine the additional stigma a male victim of sexual assault faces when choosing whether or not to come forward for medical attention, or to pursue a criminal case.

Most men under these circumstances would not want to face hospital personnel or police and go through the physical or interview processes and other challenges. I was put in a unique position with these calls. I was basically the first person each of them talked about the assault. I would have an enormous impact on how safe they would feel and whether or not they would choose to take it any further.

This would not be the only time I would find myself at this particular crossroads—being given an opportunity to make someone feel safe enough to share their story, and if I did it well, it could affect the rest of their life and healing. They could go on to feel safe enough to keep telling it to others, and to feel no shame. They had a right to reclaim their life and happiness, and this could be the beginning of that process if I did a good enough job making them feel safe and heard. This paragraph summarizes what I love about advocacy. It not only offers people an opportunity to make their situation better by using the tools and information available to them—it also reminds them that they are worth fighting for.

Maybe it is a child seeing a parent speak out on their behalf. Or a friend speaking up for another friend and demanding that she be treated with respect while out for drinks. Maybe it is someone having the worst moment of their life, and somehow, they take the time out to notice that there is a complete stranger there for them, just to advocate on their behalf. No personal motivation or agenda, simply there for whatever they need. In that moment, I would hope that the person who has experienced trauma realizes that they deserve better. And the person sitting next to them is the witness to that, and maybe can be the person who helps them begin to build something better going forward.

My early experience with male victims came in handy again later during my years as coordinator when I had a male volunteer who wanted to become a victim advocate. This was going to require some thought and planning, but I really wanted to make this happen, if I actually had a man who cared enough to make this kind of an impact on someone's life. He was a well-established volunteer in other parts of our volunteer program, so we already knew him quite well. We knew we would need to be prepared whenever he was on call, in case he responded to a call and a victim was not comfortable having a male advocate.

So, every time I would put him on the schedule, I put a female advocate on as his back-up. If he got to the hospital and a victim was uncomfortable having him as the advocate, this volunteer would call the back-up. This never had to be implemented. He was a wonderful advocate, and it was an enormous bit of diversity and a new perspective that our program benefited from greatly. He continued with us as a volunteer until the time he moved out of state.

The more practice I got on callouts, the more confident I became. I became very comfortable in the role, and comfortable standing up and demanding justice for others (or at least medical care and healthy options, depending on what they needed and wanted to do). It was always completely up to them what they did. The experience I got from working with victims and survivors was invaluable. It is something that is very hard to put into words, but doing it for a long period of time makes you (or most of us) absolutely certain and confident that **you are doing the right thing, any time you are speaking up, stepping up or fighting for someone who cannot speak for themselves.**

A lot of people who are victims of these crimes have been marginalized by society for most of their lives. It has been ingrained in them that they don't matter. And as sad and unjust as that is, we can't ignore that it is their true experience. So experiencing being a victim of a crime (if they even see it as such) is nothing new.

Sometimes. it takes someone from the outside coming in to gently point out, "This is not supposed to happen," "It is not normal for people to abuse and hurt you," and "*You deserve better.*" But perhaps the hardest one, "You have to believe that you deserve better and expect it, and then accept nothing less." Maybe I would be the first person to give them the idea that they deserved more. But with any luck, if I referred them for counseling or advocacy services, I would not be the last.

I was frequently the person who might introduce to them that this was an opportunity for them to make a change and expect, even demand more for their life. I knew all too well that someone doesn't change their whole life after spending one night at the ER with a stranger, just because "she said so." I wasn't going to be able to undo a lifetime of pain, trauma, and abuse. But I might be able to be a person in that moment (or six or seven hours) who truly cared, without expecting anything in return. No ulterior motive, nothing to be gained personally, just looking out for them and their needs. For many, this could be the first time they were having such an experience. And I began to realize what an incredible opportunity it was to be able to impress upon someone in crisis that they could work towards something more.

But the beliefs that many may have been taught since they were born are not going to be "undone" easily. These are things that abused children have been told or taught since birth,-They include messages like:

- You are not good enough.

- You don't matter.

- Your needs don't matter.

- I am the adult, and you are the child, so I matter more.

- I am bigger, stronger, more powerful, so I take what I want.

Chapter 12
My Philosophy in Training and Supervising Victim Advocates

After several years of volunteering for this role, the current volunteer coordinator for the Sexual Assault Program was leaving her position. I had never felt more suited for any job, and I was ready to get back to working outside the home. I interviewed for the position, and after a tough second interview, I was hired for the position. There were so many things about this role that made it a unique and incredible opportunity, not the least of which were the people I encountered, who were now the volunteers I was responsible for training and supervising. This was a daunting task, because this was such an exceptional group of people.

I worked with this amazing group of volunteers for over ten years, and it brought me so much joy and so many challenges. I have been told, and I agree, that being surrounded by such an outstanding group of amazing people may have tainted my expectations for the rest of the people out there in the world. It definitely caused me to have high expectations of other people, which certainly not everyone lived up to. To be fair, it takes an exceptional person to be willing to give of themselves in this way for no pay, in the middle of the night, knowing the emotional toll it would take. This was an "after-hours" schedule, which meant that any time after five p.m., overnight, and throughout the weekend, if a call came to the hospital for a victim, a volunteer would be the one to respond.

Over the years, I was accused by both my supervisor and our executive director of being very tough on new volunteers. That was the absolute truth. I did not feel that just anyone could do this role, simply because they wanted to. Good intentions alone did not qualify someone to be a victim advocate.

Unfortunately, one of the things that frequently draws people to this role is having their own experience as a victim. As you would expect, it takes years of intense work with a qualified therapist to work through your own history with sexual assault or abuse in order to serve as a victim advocate without it triggering your own experience, or without it being about you instead of the person you are there to help.

This is a particularly difficult issue to navigate with new volunteers. My philosophy was always to screen sexual assault survivors during the interview process extensively. We needed to explore their own history with these issues to see if they were at a place where they could do this work in a healthy way, and one that would not interfere with their own mental health, or the mental well-being of the person they would be seeing at the hospital. If they were not ready for the role, I would address it head on, and refer them for counseling so that they could immediately address their unresolved issues. The volunteer role was not the place to do this, and it would only cause harm to them and others if they pursued it at that time.

Sometimes I would get into trouble with my supervisor over this one, as she felt it was also a function of my role as volunteer coordinator to screen and refer people to our counseling program. Many times, she would suggest that I allow someone to go through the training program, and then tell them—after twenty hours of classroom training and giving up two entire weekends to learn these new skills—that they were going to be referred to our counseling program instead. My preference was, with those people who I knew needed counseling first, to refer them for it immediately, and encourage them to pursue the advocate role later.

This was not a popular approach, with either my supervisor or the prospective volunteers. But it was far more compassionate not to waste their time and get their hopes up, when I knew within an hour of meeting them, they weren't ready for the role. My primary concern always had to be the people we were serving, not the feelings of people who wanted to be volunteers. And the more experience I gained in interviewing and assessing prospective volunteers, the more confident I was in my approach. If someone "needed" to do this role in order to heal their trauma—what they really needed was more therapy.

Sadly, in many instances, such individuals were trying to resolve their own issues about sexual assault and abuse by applying as a volunteer. Going on callouts with victims at the ER is not a healthy or appropriate way to do this. And it was unkind to mislead them, so I would refuse to do it. By now, I had enough experience in the supervisor role to be confident in my evaluation of someone after interviewing them.

When we got to the role-play portion of the training, this would usually reveal all the major red flags that the other trainers and I would see in people. We always structured the role-plays to be held on two different days, and each time the person would have a different group facilitator. I would rely heavily on my "trainer volunteers" to help evaluate who was ready, who was not, who was just nervous, who was just not getting it, and occasionally, who was there for all the wrong reasons or was inappropriate.

Chapter 13
Sexual Assault Volunteer Training

It probably sounds odd, but there was nothing I enjoyed more than doing the volunteer training. I had been helping the former coordinator of the program with volunteer training for a number of years already, so by the time I assumed the role of supervising the program, I felt reasonably confident about how the training should go.

I was never inclined towards being a teacher, but I excelled in this role and at teaching these particular skills. If you came to us as an empathetic person with a genuine desire to help, barring any personal conflicts, we would be able to turn you into a volunteer victim advocate in about thirty hours. I was fully aware that I was solely responsible for the type of volunteers we ended up with in the program, and I was going to make sure that they were all excellent. Each of these people had to be someone I would feel comfortable with if I were the victim at the ER, or if it was someone I loved who needed extra care and attention.

The training was divided into parts. Here are just a few that were always included:

- Introduction/ice-breaker/intro to the role of advocate
- Dynamics of domestic violence (DV) and sexual assault (SA)
- Myths and realities of DV and SA
- Paperwork
- The role of the advocate
- Taking care of yourself as an advocate
- Compensation available for crime victims through the state/application process
- Sexual Assault Nurse Examiners (SANE)—the role and the process of the exam
- Video of a sample callout

- Active listening definition, explanation, and exercise with a partner

- HIV meds, pregnancy prevention, STI (Sexually Transmitted Infections) prevention and screening

- Role-plays of real cases

- Self-care

- Secondary trauma (for instance, being exposed to people who have been traumatized themselves, or disturbing descriptions of traumatic events by a survivor)

- What you will need: callout bag with clothes, paperwork, etc.

- How to report your call-out activity from your shift

- Ongoing training and supervision requirements

- Pairing up with trainer volunteers

Chapter 14
An Emotionally Draining Role:
Secondary Trauma

Despite all this dedication and passion for the work, it was incredibly emotionally draining and difficult work. It can't be ignored that we were there bearing witness to people's intense trauma. There is such a thing as secondary trauma, also known as vicarious trauma, and I tried to never forget that. I needed to always be aware that at any time, a volunteer might need an immediate break.

Secondary trauma can be experienced when an individual is exposed to people who have been traumatized themselves, as well as disturbing descriptions of traumatic events by a survivor. Symptoms of secondary trauma are similar to those of PTSD (intrusive re-experiencing of the traumatic material, avoidance of trauma triggers/emotions, negative changes in beliefs and feelings, and hyperarousal). Secondary trauma has been researched in first responders, nurses and doctors, mental health care workers, and children of traumatized parents.

To be honest, there were certain Mondays I couldn't easily face going to work. We always received more calls during the weekend, and I would call in to a "back door" phone number where the volunteers would call to report their callout activity by leaving me a voicemail. Some Mondays, I would call and brace myself to hear the number of messages that had been left for me. I would sometimes hold my breath when I called that number only to hear, "You have thirteen new messages," This was an indicator that there had been several different callouts, and probably a couple of messages per each one to leave me all the essential details. There was no way around it, this was a lot of secondary traumas to absorb, and I would feel it.

More importantly, the volunteer who was actually in that room with the victim for five to eight hours was really feeling it. And I needed to be the first line of defense in making sure the volunteers were taken care of. I took this more seriously than any part of the job, other than the quality of service that the victims received. It certainly always came first over things like paperwork and other requirements. These volunteers were our front-line workers, and I wanted them to be cared for and appreciated.

When the program was doing well, I had over thirty volunteers to schedule, train, supervise, and keep happy. Don't forget that last one. Remember that they were volunteers; they could leave at any time if they were not satisfied. We also required them to receive ongoing training on several topics relevant to their role as a victim advocate. We would have police officers from the Abused Persons' Unit, a nurse from the Sexual Assault Nurse Examiners, and one of our educators who worked with kids in schools about prevention of sexual abuse. Other topics included elder abuse, the district attorney's office, abuse among special populations, review of filling out the application for compensation from the state for expenses related to the crime, etc. We had monthly meetings with the volunteers to stay in touch, do these continued in-service trainings, and check in about their recent callouts.

There was also great satisfaction in maintaining a strong number of volunteers staying on as volunteers for several years, and many of them wanting to do more, like serving as trainer volunteers and helping with volunteer training. Trainer volunteers go out on a call with a newly trained volunteer until they are comfortable to be on their own. Volunteers help with training in a number of ways: assisting with presentations, answering questions for attendees, running role-play groups, and assessing new volunteers' suitability for the role at the conclusion of training. They were an integral part of making the decision which attendees could move on to have the role of victim advocate. This was not particularly glamorous work and included helping with the nitty-gritty like picking up lunch and cleaning the kitchen, in addition to all the functional parts of the training material itself, and yet they would consistently volunteer their weekends to do it, year after year. I must have been doing something right. They were just as dedicated as I was.

We had a strong and consistent group of trainers whom I could call upon each year to help with training. They were in charge of the kitchen, would each take on a role-play group to facilitate, would help me keep the agenda moving on time, keep an eye out for anyone who seemed to be struggling or could be triggered by the training content, and most importantly, they would contribute to the discussion of each topic and help me evaluate each trainee at the end of the process.

Chapter 15
Leaving the Role, or So I Thought

During the years I worked for the women's agency, I had really been in my element. And while the role was demanding, I absolutely loved it. It was difficult, but so fulfilling. I never once doubted that I was absolutely making a difference. It was a role I hoped to keep for years to come.

Eventually, however, a new opportunity came along as my husband and I set our sights on moving out of state to a warmer climate when he retired. I took a part-time job with Delta, mainly to receive the flight benefits. I had never been drawn to that type of work, but it was a means to an end. The biggest plus to it was the people I met there and came to love.

A couple of years after accepting the Delta job, I decided to leave the women's agency to focus on only one work schedule up until the time we were ready to move. Little did I know that when I left this job, the role would never truly leave me. I would be called back years later to protest the actions of this agency, which had once become my second home. They might one day regret having taught me to become such a fierce and relentless advocate.

It was now an integral part of me to always fight for what was right and for who needed to be spoken for. I also found that survivors and those in need of advocacy continued to seek me out in a number of ways and settings.

Chapter 16
Self-Care

Self-care means taking the time to do things that help you live well and improve both your physical and mental health. When it comes to your mental health, self-care can help manage stress, lower your risk of illness, and increase your energy. Even small acts of self-care in your daily life can have a big impact.

There is no question that one of the most critical parts of being able to do this kind of work for any substantial period of time is self-care. The list below was compiled from information from the National Institute of Mental Health's website (*nimh.nih.gov*).

Here are some tips to help you get started with self-care:

- **Get regular exercise.** Just a short bit of exercise each day can help boost your mood and improve your health. Small amounts of exercise add up, so don't think that a few minutes a day is not enough to matter.

- **Eat healthy, regular meals and stay hydrated.** A balanced diet and plenty of water improves your energy and focus throughout the day.

- **Make sleep a priority.** Stick to a schedule, and make sure you are getting plenty of sleep.

- **Try a relaxing activity.** Explore relaxation and wellness programs or apps which may incorporate meditation, muscle relaxation, or breathing exercises. Schedule regular time for these and other healthy activities, such as journaling.

- **Set goals and priorities.** Decide what must get done and what can wait. Learn to say "no" to tasks if you start to feel like you are taking on too much. Be mindful of all that you have accomplished by the end of the day, not what you did not complete.

- **Practice gratitude.** Remind yourself daily of the things you are grateful for. Be specific, write them down, and keep a gratitude journal if you find it helpful.

- **Focus on positivity.** Identify and challenge your negative and unhelpful thoughts.

- **Stay connected**. Reach out to family and friends who can provide emotional support and practical help.

Self-care looks different for everyone. You will need to find what works for you, and what causes or triggers mild symptoms and anxiety for you. You will figure out what coping techniques work to help you manage symptoms. You will need to remember that if you are an advocate in a role where you are a first responder, you are therefore susceptible to secondary trauma, also known as vicarious trauma. You will need to learn and practice what works for you to cope and maintain a healthy emotional and mental state.

This will be an ongoing and fluid process. You may find that the same activities or practices don't always work in the same way. Have a list ready, and keep a journal of your thoughts as well as what activities work for you to reestablish your sense of mental well-being.

These things will take time to complete. You will need to allow for this and give yourself permission to take this time out of your busy schedule. This is just as important as your physical health. Mental health is part of your physical health. Choosing a role that takes a mental toll on you requires you to prioritize taking care of yourself. You matter too, and it is just like what they tell you when you get on the airplane: "You have to put your own oxygen mask on first before you can assist someone else." If you aren't getting oxygen, you will be in no position to help others. You also want to be at your best not just for yourself, but for your family. If you are the type of person who wants to care for others, sometimes strangers you don't even know, it is fair to assume that you give a great deal to your own family and friends also.

Make sure you have at least one person in your life who you can turn to when you need time to unload on someone else. People get used to you being the giver, the listener, the helpful one. You will need to make it clear that you have needs too. Some people are very good at this, and others are not. Sometimes people assume that you don't need anyone because you always appear to be strong. Of course, that isn't true, but it is necessary for you to remind people of this from time to time. Doing so is not selfish; it is the very definition of self-care. When you aren't practicing self-care or let things build up, they will blow at the very worst possible moment.

Some of my most useful self-care practices are listed here. Remember, you will need to explore and find out what works for you.

- Shopping/going out to eat
- Doing something out of your routine
- Taking a drive
- Getting out of town
- ICE CREAM
- Talking to a friend
- Creating art, even if you are not good
- Scribbling, painting vigorously, breaking glass
- Baking
- Coloring
- Journaling
- Getting regular exercise

III.
Survivor Interviews, Part 2

Chapter 17
Chris

A neighbor and friend reached out to us one day when I was still working as a victim advocate/coordinator of the Sexual Assault Volunteer Program. My husband was a state trooper, and she knew about my experience as an advocate. She needed advice that we both could offer her. Her husband had become physically abusive, and he was blaming it all on her.

She was terrified, embarrassed, and did not know what to do next. But the prospect of ending her long-term marriage did not seem like an option. She had called the police and they had filed a report, but her husband was already working on getting back into their home, while she felt strongly, they needed to separate immediately. As I said, he was blaming her with brilliant statements like, "You are the only one who makes me do this." She turned to me, and tried to make sense of what was happening.

I explained to her that even though I was a domestic violence advocate, for her I would not be taking on that same role. Domestic violence advocates are neutral, they give all the control to the person in the situation who needs to make the decisions, and they present options, not opinions.

I was not "neutral" here, and I needed to let her know that from the beginning. For her, I would be a good friend with the knowledge of an advocate, but I would be sharing my opinions freely, and my main goal was keeping her safe (not giving her all the control in the decision-making process as I would as an advocate). I would be challenging all the faulty statements her husband had been feeding her in the process of blaming her for his being abusive.

I have been in this situation more than once with friends. Step one is making sure they are safe. Step two is letting them know that I will not be neutral, leaving all choices up to them or checking my opinions at the door. It is very difficult to know what I should be saying and doing as an advocate in a situation with a friend, but then I feel my personality and true self come through and take over as I deal with the person as my friend, not as I would act if she were a client. I am sure that, more than once, I was overbearing by allowing my true self to take over, but I would be making sure that my friends and acquaintances survived their abusive partners, and nothing—not even the importance of them reclaiming their control—would take priority over that with someone I knew and cared about.

When my neighbor Chris talked about some of her husband's behaviors that had been a part of their whole marriage, it was obvious that his controlling and abusive tendencies had always been there. But I felt like this was a new realization for her, so I was trying to introduce this idea to her gently. This was going to hit her like a train when it finally sank in that this was not a new problem, just one that had finally come to a head.

One day I said to her, "Does this even make sense that he is blaming you for his behavior? Does that work both ways? Can you blame him for your behavior? Have you ever done that?" She had to admit that the answer was no. We would go through stages where she would call me to talk, and then there would be a break in the length of time since we had talked. What I kept reminding myself was that statistic that it takes a woman, on average, eight times of leaving an abusive relationship before they can leave it for good.

During one of those breaks of time from talking to her, something else occurred to me. The next time she called me, I shared it with her. I told her that I knew that what I usually had to say to her was so hard for her to hear, yet she kept coming back to me to hear it or ask advice. I thought she knew that I was telling her the truth, and what she knew she needed to hear, no matter how much she disliked it. I said that I felt she was slowly realizing that she needed to eventually believe and internalize the things I had been telling her.

He wasn't going to change. It would always be her fault, in his mind. He would never share any of the blame. And probably most importantly, I suspected that he didn't even see anything wrong with his behavior, and he never would. She moved on to divorce him, and to move out of the area and eventually to remarry. She is much happier now, and free of his abusive behavior. Her current husband treats her like a queen.

When I told Chris I was planning to write this book, she sent me these comments to include: "I knew Karen as a friend and neighbor; there came a time I was thankful to have her as an advocate. As a victim of domestic violence, and not realizing that is what it was, I reached out to Karen one morning, and without hesitation she talked with me and helped me through one of the hardest things I've had to do. Step by step, giving me the guidance and encouragement to move forward."

Chapter 18
Emotional and Physical Effects of Keeping Silent

Not speaking out can have serious effects on a survivor. *KMDLaw.com* reports the numerous results that can come from keeping silent about abuse:

- Having flashbacks of the event

- Trouble connecting with loved ones, romantic partners, and co-workers

- Emotional outbursts of anger

- Feeling moody, anxious or sad

- Feeling overwhelmed or irritable

- Heightened sensitivity to certain noises or smells

- Trouble sleeping or concentrating

- Change in appetite

- Not wanting to do the activities once enjoyed

- Increased headaches, nausea, or chest pain

Chapter 19
Lauren Marie

I was connected with Lauren Marie when her mom, Tammy, saw that I was looking for people to interview for this book. Tammy was one of my best and most dedicated volunteers when I worked at the Center for Survivors of Sexual Assault and Domestic Violence. She was so compassionate and dedicated. I was so sad to learn that her daughter had experienced a sexual assault in the military. I soon realized that Lauren Marie had inherited her mother's convictions and tenacity. Thank you so much to both of you.

Lauren Marie's Voice

I was sexually assaulted in the military and sought out a victim advocate. It helped me with the legal aspects of opening an unrestricted report, as well as helping me with the legal process in general. I was part of the "Teal Rope" program, which is a military program to support survivors of sexual assault. A teal rope, when worn around the shoulder of an airman's uniform, designates the training and volunteerism the student has undergone to be able to assist peers in dealing with sexual assault. The primary objective is to promote a climate of respect, dignity, and professionalism. It makes resources available to students while increasing awareness. Because I was in this program as a trained advocate, I knew exactly where to go when I needed help.

I always knew that I could go to my advocate when I couldn't get into the mental health services to see someone. My advocate definitely taught me how I needed to talk to legal representatives/officials, how to explain what had happened to me in a way that they were looking for, and she explained the whole process to me. I was able to register my perpetrator with the "catch program," which would allow him to be highlighted if another case with another victim came up where the description of the perpetrator met his description.

Thankfully, I knew who to go to in terms of finding an advocate when I was assaulted. I know that I would not have chosen to come forward to report my assault without an advocate's support. I would have kept quiet about what happened to me, because I knew there were a lot more people who would be against me than those who would support me in coming forward.

If someone you know goes through something like this, I would advise the people who are close to them to just be there and comfort them. That is what I needed most. Even if we weren't talking about it, both my friend and my advocate were just there for me. Make an effort to be there, and make it known that you are there and that you care. My friend had had a similar experience, and she was already empowered, so she encouraged me to talk about my experience. Everything around me was closing me down, and she showed me how to be strong in that moment.

My perpetrator had shown me clear signs that he had no intentions of taking any accountability for what he had done to me. He had a lot of power and money, and he was not afraid to use that to get what he needed. He had shown me this in another instance when we were in a car accident together where he was the driver. He refused to report the accident and didn't want me to get the medical treatment that I really needed. So I documented everything, in preparation for what I would need to do next. I definitely felt shame, because part of the assault had been recorded, and people were coming to me asking me about it.

Initially I didn't even tell my mom for about two weeks. I didn't want to put her and my dad through all the pain that it would cause them. But my mom could tell something was going on, and I eventually told her. There are things that were caused by the assault, like me having PTSD, that really upset me. But I have a stronger head on my shoulders now than before this happened.

For people going through something similar, I would want them to know that they can talk about it out in the open, and they should. Especially in the military. It still goes unnoticed and is not discussed. In this male-dominated culture, so many things are just dismissed without them even being brought to any kind of review. People need to be able to talk about it in the open, not keeping it hush-hush.

Recently one of my superiors told me and another person a rape joke. I called him out on it, saying that if he said that to someone else, they might not be as forgiving as I was. I told him I wanted him to be accountable, and he apologized to both of us. I hope this makes him pause next time, before saying something inappropriate.

I lost a lot of friendships over this assault. A lot of people took the man's side and even went to go so far as telling my mom that I was going crazy. They told me they had warned me not to hang out with him. It's really important that you are aware of what someone is going through and that you're capable of having an adult conversation about it. You need to surround yourself with the right kind of supportive people, and that will not include everyone who is currently in your life.

Chapter 20
Overcoming Victim-Blaming

Victims frequently encounter the following statements or questions and many more. This list was compiled and published on the *KMDLaw.com* site:

- Why didn't you run away or fight back?

- Why didn't you file a police report?

- Why are you just bringing this up now after all these years?

- Were you drinking alcohol when it happened?

- You led them on, that is why this happened.

- What did you expect to happen?

- You should have been more careful.

- Look at what you are wearing, you were asking for it.

- How could this have happened with your mother in the house?

- Why isn't anyone else coming forward?

- I never saw anything.

- There would have been signs.

- I have no reason to believe you over him.

- How do you know they are accurate if they were repressed memories?

Chapter 21
Jen

I first met Jen when working at the agency for survivors. She was very active in our group of survivors and had also become a victim advocate in a local agency for children that our agency partnered with. We had occasion to work together sometimes and collaborate, as our agencies worked closely together. She was also a major voice of support for survivors in the community during the protest of the agency I formerly worked for, which you will read more about later. Thank you, Jen, for your strength, your voice, and sharing your story.

Jen's Voice

Can you tell me a little bit about the life circumstances that caused you to seek out the help of a DV/SA advocate (if you did)?

I was raped at the age of eighteen, and I did not tell anyone until over a year and a half later. I did not have an advocate.

In what ways did having an advocate make a difference in your situation?

I think things would have been a lot different if I had an advocate after I was raped. I was too afraid to tell anyone for fear of not being believed and fear of being judged.

Try to describe the difference it makes to have someone advocating or being there for you.

I can't speak for myself in having an advocate, but I can speak for myself as someone who also worked as an advocate. Having someone who can be in your corner as a support person and someone who can guide you is an invaluable connection. It is something that I didn't know existed at the time that I was raped, and I felt compelled to be that person for others in my work later on in my life because it was something that I didn't have and something that I so desperately needed at the time.

What difference does that support make in a situation like yours?

I think that if I had that support, my road to healing would have been a lot different. In experiencing rape, which is very often an isolating experience, having someone who can listen, provide support, and offer referrals and resources to assistance helps set a survivor on the right path in healing. I didn't have anyone at the time, and I was very isolated and alone.

Do you ever think about how your life might be different if you hadn't had that support?

I think my life would have been a lot different if I had support. When I first sought help, I was met with questions such as, "What did you think was going to happen since you went back to his apartment?" This was by a school therapist. Responses like that only continue to breed shame and blame on the victim, who probably already has those feelings!

Eventually, I ended up at a local agency for counseling, and that was a life-changing experience since I was finally being believed and helped. If I had that after the assault first happened, I think I would have been in a completely different place emotionally. Even eighteen years later, I still hear therapists' words of judgment.

What advice would you give to someone who had a family member or close friend come forward to disclose their abuse or assault to you?

Saying, "I believe you. It wasn't your fault. How can I help?" Offering support is the biggest and most helpful thing anyone can do. Offering to listen and to be there if the person needs it. Don't force them to talk about it, but offer to listen if they would like to talk.

What difference does that first person's reaction make? Positive? Negative?

Huge. The first person I talked to listened and held me as I cried. After that, the responses weren't very positive, including when I sought out professional help from a therapist. I will always remember the positive response and also the negative response. Truthfully, I find the negative response to be more in the forefront of my thoughts, though. So I think it really is very important to be met with a loving reaction.

What were some obstacles that kept you from reaching out for help sooner?

I was eighteen, alone in my first month of college as a freshman. I didn't have many friends yet. My family didn't like that I was dating this guy. I was worried that I was going to be met with "I told you so" and people saying that it was my fault. It took me a really long time to be able to say anything. I was able to push my thoughts and feelings away for over a year and live my life as if nothing had happened. Until I couldn't do that anymore. After that, I realized how much I needed help.

Did you ever feel shame or embarrassment about your situation? And if so, why do you think that is, since you had done nothing wrong?

Absolutely. My rapist made sure he found ways to humiliate me. It caused me to feel a lot of shame that was perpetuated by people who didn't believe me and who blamed me for what had happened. I still struggle with shame sometimes, but this is something I am working on.

Were there specific people in your life you couldn't or wouldn't tell? Why?

I was afraid to tell a lot of my family and close friends because I was ashamed.

What was it about their reaction that you feared?

I was afraid that they would blame me. I also feared that by telling people that I was closest to, that I would cause them pain, or they would look at me differently.

How is your life different now from when you were in an abusive relationship or once you began to heal from your abuse/assault?

Now, I am in a loving relationship, married, and have children. I think healing is always evolving, and I continue to go to therapy to work on my healing.

What are the major differences?

I wasn't really in an abusive relationship with my abuser. He was a casual boyfriend at the time, and I did not see him again after he assaulted me. I feel safe with my husband and that is the biggest thing for me.

What else would you want someone reading this book to know?

I think it's extremely important to meet someone where they are and not force them to talk if they aren't ready. I also think that the most imperative thing you can do is to be supportive and to listen lovingly and without judgment.

Did you ever feel judged or unsafe to tell people close to you?

Yes. I think that is why I didn't talk about it for a really long time. I was made to feel like I was "too much," and my needs were "too much." The therapist had already blamed me for what happened. I felt deep shame, and therefore, I didn't feel safe enough to talk about it.

What could they have done better that would have made a difference to you?

Listened without judgment. Provided support and care in ways that I needed instead of judging.

Chapter 22
Assumptions Survivors Encounter

Survivors who come forward about sexual abuse or assault usually face challenging and cruel assumptions, which often place the onus of wrongdoing on them rather than on the abuser, where it belongs.

In a *PBS.org* article, writer Judy Woodruff discussed a "... cultural predisposition to perpetuate a lot of rape myths: one of those being that women excessively exaggerate and/or make things up. There are misinterpretations .... Our culture in general attributes lying to women who come forward." Woodruff also pointed out, "There is a generational change in some contexts. Younger women are really leading the way in terms of being more comfortable about speaking up than that of the previous generation."

According to the article from PBS, the following are assumptions frequently encountered by women coming forward about sexual assault or abuse allegations.

- You have to defend what you have said happened to you, maybe even by giving specifics in order for some to understand or believe you.

- You are being questioned about what and how you remember and what you say you remember.

- Survivors fear being shamed, blamed and there is fear of retaliation, and of being doubted. In addition, there is fear of victim-blaming, of not being believed, and of being shunned.

- Survivors have been conditioned by the perpetrator to keep silent, or brainwashed to believe that the abuse was their fault, so they blame themselves and fear retaliation and fear that they will have no support or place to turn for help.

Women will always pay a huge price for coming forward: including but not limited to disbelief, scrutiny, bullying, even death threats if the accused is a powerful man. They can expect to be accused of lying and/or having their credibility questioned. People would rather believe anything than believe that this person, the perpetrator, could have harmed a child.

IV.
Domestic Violence, Sexual Assault and Trauma

Chapter 23
Domestic Violence and Sexual Assault

While this book is full of my opinions, I also want it to include important facts, as well as suggestions for where you can learn more. Information in this chapter was collected from:

- Domestic Abuse Intervention Programs, Home of the Duluth Model, Duluth, MN | *theduluthmodel.org*

- Rape Abuse Incest National Network (RAINN), Washington, DC | *RAINN.org*

- Joyful Heart Foundation | *joyfulheartfoundation.org*

- Children's Assessment Center, Houston, TX | *CACHouston.org*

- National Institute of Mental Health (NIMH) *nimh.nih.gov*

- One of the most widely used theories regarding domestic violence is the Duluth Model, including the Power and Control Wheel (see more about this in the Appendix). This model has been used to explain the dynamics of domestic violence in a way that is easy to understand. It is used by most domestic violence agencies throughout the country.

Examples of abusive behavior can be easily identified and found on the Power and Control Wheel. It is characterized by the pattern of actions that an individual uses to intentionally control or dominate his/her intimate partner. The complement to this is the Equality Wheel.

Power and Control Wheel

DOMESTIC ABUSE INTERVENTION PROGRAMS
202 East Superior Street
Duluth, Minnesota 55802
218-722-2781
www.theduluthmodel.org

Equality Wheel

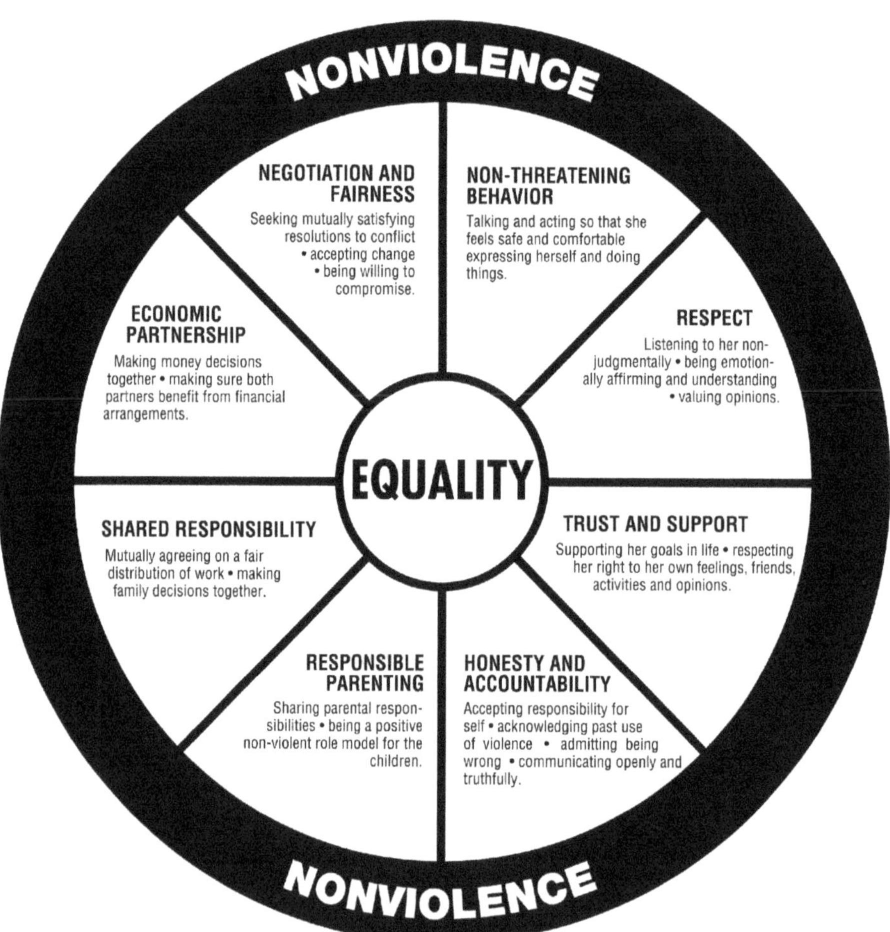

DOMESTIC ABUSE INTERVENTION PROGRAMS
202 East Superior Street
Duluth, Minnesota 55802
218-722-2781
www.theduluthmodel.org

The following are just a few general facts and statistics compiled regarding domestic violence, child sexual abuse, and sexual assault:

- The majority of sexual assault victims are under thirty, with 54 percent of all victims falling between the ages of eighteen and thirty-four. Younger people are at the highest risk of sexual violence.

- Every sixty-eight seconds, an American is sexually assaulted.

- One out of every six American women has been the victim of attempted or completed rape.

- Men and boys are also affected by sexual violence.

- Many women will not identify what they are experiencing as domestic violence, especially if there has not been physical violence.

- Transgender students are at higher risk of sexual violence.

- Approximately 70 percent of sexual assault victims experience moderate to severe distress, a larger percentage than any other crime.

- Many women will not believe that their partner will physically harm them because the partner has not done so in the past. What they may not recognize is that everything changes when a partner begins to lose control over the woman.

- Almost 80 percent of survivors who were victimized by a family member, close friend, or acquaintance experience professional or emotional issues, including moderate to severe distress, or increased problems at work or school.

- False allegations of rape are extremely rare. In fact, most people who are raped or experience another form of sexual violence never tell the police. The rate of "false reports" is minimal (under two percent), equal to the rate of false reports of other crimes.

- Many survivors of rape or sexual violence are unable to come forward, for fear of not being believed, fear of being judged or blamed. The shame victims experience is crippling and long lasting. There is also fear of their perpetrator finding out and lashing out at them.

- Family structure is the most important risk factor in child sexual abuse. Children who live with two married biological parents are at low risk for abuse. The risk increases when children live with stepparents or a single parent. Children living without either parent (foster children) are ten times more likely to be sexually abused than children who live with both biological parents. Children who live with a single parent who has a live-in partner are at highest risk: they are twenty times more likely to be the victims of child sexual abuse than children living with both biological parents. (Sedlack, et al., 2010)

- Age is a significant factor in sexual abuse. While there is risk for children of all ages, children are most vulnerable to abuse between the ages of seven and thirteen. (Finkelhor, 1994)

- Most child sexual abusers are men and may be respected members of the community drawn to settings where they gain easy access to children like schools, clubs, and churches. Most victims know and trust their abusers, who come from all age groups, races, religions, and socioeconomic classes.

Chapter 24
A Few Facts About Trauma

The word trauma literally means wound, shock, or injury. Psychological trauma is a person's experience of emotional distress resulting from an event that overwhelms the capacity to emotionally digest it.

As a recent article in *Psychology Today* explains, "Traumatic experiences undermine a person's sense of safety in the world and create a sense that catastrophe could strike at any time. Any sudden, violent disruption—such as parental loss in childhood, car accidents, physical violence, sexual assault, military combat experiences, earthquakes, and the unexpected loss of a loved one—are events that can lead to trauma. The experience leads to changes in brain function that causes hypersensitivity to threats."

There are several types of traumas, effects of trauma, and treatments for trauma. Information from The University of Northern Colorado's website describes how trauma or extreme fear alters brain chemistry, and how this can affect survivors of sexual assaults or abuse:

"This is called the 'Fear Circuitry,' and it is the protective mechanism which we all have inside of us. The neurobiology of trauma—the effects of trauma on the brain—is important to understand because it helps break down the common misconceptions and victim-blaming about gender-based violence and it helps survivors to understand their experience and aftermath in a new way.

"*Dissociation* is a survival reflex where someone may feel disconnected from their body. They may feel they go outside of their body and go on 'auto-pilot' mode. In auto-pilot mode, a person is not using their pre-frontal cortex to make decisions, but instead is relying on habitual modes of being. Habitual responses are based on how we were socialized to behave. Women are socialized to be polite and pleasing to 'save face,' placate, or keep the peace. This means that during an assault, a person might engage in sexual acts, say polite things, or even smile. This does not mean that they are consenting. They are actually experiencing extreme fear and their brain is operating on auto-pilot as a survival mechanism.

"Memories are encoded differently during a traumatic event. The brain does not encode memories in chronological order, there are gaps in memory, and whatever the 'fear circuitry' in the brain focused attention on during the assault is more likely to be encoded into memory than periphery details. For example, a survivor may remember the exact smell of the perpetrator's cologne, but not have any memory of what the room looked like."

Chapter 25
Eye Movement Desensitization and Reprocessing (EMDR)

A psychotherapy treatment called EMDR, or Eye Movement Desensitization and Reprocessing, is an essential tool that can be used to help so many people who suffer so greatly from traumatic experiences.

The EMDR Institute website, EMDR.com, discusses how, with the help of a trained specialist, survivors can use EMDR to find relief from the emotional distress symptoms resulting from trauma.

"The techniques can be used during the process when a person is trying to recall details of traumatic events that may have been repressed as a way that brain acted to protect the person in the moments when the trauma was occurring. These memories must be brought back slowly and carefully so as not to re-traumatize the person who experienced the events.

"The brain is an amazing thing and has incredible powers to protect us from harm, as well as having a natural process of moving towards mental health. But when this system is blocked or imbalanced by the impact of a disturbing event, the emotional wound festers and can cause intense suffering. Once the block is removed, healing resumes.

"In successful EMDR therapy, the meaning of painful events is transformed on an emotional level. For instance, a rape victim shifts from feeling self-disgust and horror to the belief that, "I survived it and am strong." The insights that clients gain in EMDR therapy result from the client's own intellectual and emotional processes. EMDR therapy results in clients feeling empowered by the experiences that once debased them. Their wounds are transformed by the process. The clients' thoughts, feelings and behavior are all robust indicators of emotional health and resolution."

I have included this critical information about EMDR in hopes that it can help someone in the way that it has helped so many survivors I know. When a child has shame about his/her abuse, he/she often isolates and even splits off into a "good" part that functions in the world and the "bad" part that holds the knowledge of the abuse. EMDR can help the adult survivor reconnect with the "bad" parts of their brain that hold the memories and truth about what happened, and then reintegrate them back together to feel more whole. The process of EMDR can do this slowly and safely, as to not re-traumatize the survivor. EMDR can also work to restore connections with positive figures in the survivor's life, who taught them to love and be loved. As a part of EMDR, to build ego strength, a qualified therapist who is trained in EMDR can tap into people from the survivor's life who are nurturing and protective so that they may be utilized to help with processing the trauma. (Niskanen)

Recently, an incident for one survivor I interviewed included her seeing her abuser unexpectedly, which had sent her into a full panic, causing her to freeze and lose track of what was happening around her. A few weeks later, after one session of EMDR—desensitizing her to coming face to face with the image of seeing her abuser—she was able to walk past him on the next occasion without incident.

Through EMDR survivors are reminded that it is possible to regain control over the situation and their reaction to it. It is a long-term goal to reach the point where the trauma isn't controlling them, and there is progress towards reaching that goal. What an amazing accomplishment to be in control of their own lives again!

Chapter 26
Six Steps to Helping a Survivor

While it is understandable that sexual assault/abuse is an uncomfortable subject, and one that most people don't have much experience with, there are some simple steps that everyone can take to help. If a survivor trusts you enough to share her story with you, do not let your being uncomfortable or unsure of what to say get in the way of making a life-changing difference to someone you care about. Believe me, any survivor will be more comforted by the fact that you reach out (even if you say the wrong thing) than if you avoid her and say nothing. And if you follow the steps below, you can't say the wrong thing. Let her know you care by reaching out in these ways.

Six Steps to Support a Survivor

This list was compiled by the Joyful Heart Foundation for the *joyfulheart.com* website:

1. Listen.

Sometimes you don't even need words or at least not a lot of words to be there for someone. Many people share that being able to tell their story to someone else lessens the weight of isolation, secrecy, and self-blame. Listening, in and of itself, is an act of love.

2. Validate.

Think about a time when you felt vulnerable or faced a crisis and think of what helped you the most. Chances are it was not a specific conversation you had, but it was the knowledge and comfort that the person or people you told were there for you, believed in you, were on your side, and were committed to supporting you through a hard time.

There are some helpful phrases you can use to show you care:

- "I'm so sorry this happened to you."
- "I believe you."
- "This is not your fault."
- "You're not alone, I'm here for you, and I'm glad you told me."

Oftentimes a survivor may feel like what happened to them is their fault. We are bombarded with victim-blaming myths and attitudes in our society, and they can sink in deeply. But no action excuses a person from hurting someone else. Violence and abuse are never the victim's fault. That responsibility and shame lie with the perpetrator. It can be helpful to communicate that gently and repeatedly.

- "Nothing you did or could have done differently makes this your fault."

- "The responsibility is on the person who hurt you."

- "No one ever has the right to hurt you."

- "I promise you didn't ask for this."

- "I know that it can feel like you did something wrong, but you did not."

- "It doesn't matter if you did or didn't, no one asks to be hurt in this way."

3. Ask what more you can do to help.
Violence and abuse are about power and control. It is vital for survivors to regain their sense of personal power. Instead of pushing someone into taking actions for which they are not ready, ask how you can support them.

4. Know where to point someone for more help.
You can best help a survivor by offering options and leaving space for them to decide where to go from there. Here are some national resources and services that can point someone to local resources:

- **Rape Abuse and Incest National Network Sexual Assault Hotline** 800.656.4673 | *www.rainn.org*

- **National Child Abuse Hotline**
  800.422.4453 | *www.childhelp.org*

- **National Domestic Violence Hotline**
  800.799.7233 | *www.ndvh.org*

- **National Teen Dating Abuse Helpline**
  800.331.9474 | *www.loveisrespect.org*

5. **Keep an open heart**.

Remind a survivor you are available should they like to talk about their experiences further. The healing journey can be a long one. It can be full of many challenging—but sometimes joyful and liberating—conversations. It can make a big difference to know that you are there to support them along the way.

6. **Finally, care for yourself**.

There is a limit to what we are able to take in and process. The stories of someone else's hardships related to a traumatic event can impact or become a part of us. This experience of secondhand trauma—often called vicarious trauma—is a human response to coming face to face with the reality of trauma and the difficulties of the human experience.

It is important to care for yourself as you support another person. You cannot be your best self in your supportive role if you find yourself too tired to listen with care and compassion or are overfilled with your own emotions in response to another's trauma. These feelings are valid. Take some time after a conversation to enjoy the outdoors or do a healthy activity that makes you feel good, as a way of re-centering yourself.

V.
Personal Background and How It All Started

Chapter 27
Personal Background and Art Therapy Program

The year after my father died, I graduated college and enrolled in a master's level certification program in art therapy. It was an incredible program but was not yet established at the college it would eventually become a part of. At this time, it was conducted as a clinical program at a residential treatment center for children and adolescents who had experienced trauma.

There were only three of us in the new program, and we took academic courses, along with carrying a full caseload of clients to work with using art therapy. I loved the program and was getting settled in my apartment. It was intense and demanding, but I felt it was a great fit for my passions of art and psychology that my undergraduate experience had hopefully prepared me for.

Over time, each student would be practicing more independently, in a variety of settings within the agency throughout Rochester, New York. As we gained more knowledge and skills, we would gain confidence to work more on our own, rather than under the immediate supervision of one of our supervisors. The further we progressed through the program, the more we would increase our caseload of clients as well as how in depth we would go with those clients.

This was a pretty intimidating task, given the level of trauma that all of the clients in the treatment center had experienced in their young lives. We had a lot to learn before we could possibly feel prepared to do them justice and truly help them. We eventually would branch out and work more independently at several of the satellite facilities affiliated with the agency. The goal was to prepare us to become practicing art therapists.

During that time, a series of frightening events began that probably should have been enough to make me leave the program and move home. The first incident was when I was approached in a store by a man I didn't know. He approached me and described the route I had just taken to the store, saying he had followed me from my apartment about seven miles away. I was afraid to go back to my apartment, so after talking to the police, I went to the site of my clinical program, where I spent the rest of the day. Then I began to get a series of obscene phone calls that were graphic and repetitive, in a way that made it seem impossible that they were random or unrelated to the other incidents that had or were about to happen to me.

One day soon after that, my car windshield was smashed while I was at the mall. At this point, my fiancé bought me a gun. We could only legally get a rifle, but at least I could feel a little better having something under my bed. Meanwhile, the obscene phone calls continued, and there were many nights I just couldn't stay in my apartment, so I would stay with a friend who still lived at home and fairly nearby.

Several months later, a series of rapes occurred throughout the city where I was living. The first several were not too close, so I wrote it off as part of living in a larger city. But the more they happened, the scarier it got, and on top of the other incidents, I felt like I was unraveling. One night I came home after dark, due to a late class, and as I got out of my car, I had the intense feeling that I was being watched. I heard a slight noise. I remember making a lot of noise with my keys so anyone who could hear me might realize I had them ready to stab at someone through my fingers. Even after being safely inside my apartment, I couldn't shake that feeling of being watched.

Then, less than a week later, there was a news crew outside my apartment window one night. I turned on the news to learn that there had been a rape at my apartment complex. I was terrified and couldn't function or move. I called my mom to tell her. I could not call my fiancé; he was in the police academy, where no calls were allowed. The next morning, I went out to get into my car, only to see the police tape across one of the garage openings right by mine. It was one of those long, big, garage units that had individual doors but were all connected. In my mind, it appeared that the rapist had gone through an open door and hidden behind a car until a prospective victim came into the garage.

The previous night, I had convinced myself that the rape victim was probably attacked far back from the building, while I had asked to have a garage close to the building when I first moved in. Anything to mentally distance myself from the terror that this could have been me. But when I walked outside and saw the police tape, that illusion was gone. The victim's garage was just a couple of spaces over from mine—so much for distancing myself from the thought that this could have been me. This really could have been me.

My fiancé was in another part of the state, and I couldn't call him until the weekend. Of course, my dad, who had always been my protector, was dead. This was the first of several major life events that I would navigate without that protection. And in that moment, I felt my father's absence as I had not yet felt it since he died. I had no doubt that if he had been alive, he would have driven to pick me up that night and had me withdraw from the program and move home. It would have been an over-reaction and I would have been angry, but I would not have been feeling his absence the way I was feeling it without him there. These had been the most difficult months of my life up to this point.

Keep in mind that throughout these months and all these frightening events, I was full-time in a therapeutic program where we were to be exploring all our own emotional issues. Self-exploration was a key component of the program, and your success was dependent on it.

Within two weeks of the crime at my apartment, I broke my lease and moved in with my high school math teacher. Yes, you read that correctly. The only person I could find to share an apartment with had a current roommate who was moving out in about seven weeks. I needed somewhere to live in the meantime, and the only other person I knew in the city was one of my favorite teachers from high school. So, I had to decide between this strange temporary living arrangement or leaving the graduate school program. My teacher and her husband were so gracious to me.

Chapter 28
A Series of Unrelated Events and Life Choices

When I finally moved into my new apartment, it was a big adjustment. My new roommate was in the art therapy program with me, so we were spending most of our time together between home and school. She had a significant trauma history, which I knew because of the personal information that we shared as part of our program. This was a bit of a trigger for both of us. She had been the victim of a sexual assault in the past, and I felt like I had narrowly escaped being a victim myself recently. But mostly, I became drawn to this issue.

Every time I moved around the city, whether with physical address changes or locations where I did various placements for my clinical program, the rapes were occurring near my new location. It was eerie and starting to seriously freak me out. I felt as though the rapist was following me. I struggled to see a way for me to continue with my program. Within a few months' time, there was the rape at my former apartment complex and at least three or four others in close proximity to my home or school.

At this point during my clinical program, one of the supervisors, a psychologist, was using terms related to my collective experiences like "traumatized," "victimized," and "stalked." It was the early 1990s, so stalking wasn't even a recognized crime yet. And still, no one, including the police, had found any evidence that any of these terrible incidents were in any way connected to each other or were being committed by the same person. I felt like I was going crazy, and that I had to be paranoid about what was happening to me. I didn't feel that I could judge what was real or what was reasonable.

How would I know if I should give up, quit school, and move home? I was in no mental state to make big decisions. What would I do if I did leave? My education was not complete yet. I had to finish what I had started. This may have been the first of many times when I would refuse to give up, as well as the first of many times I would refuse to become a victim—not the victim of a crime, and not the victim of a cluster of bad circumstances trying to force me to quit.

Before long, it was time to choose a topic for my thesis. This would be my entire focus for months and would be a huge part of my final grade point average for the program. I was already surrounded and consumed by the subject of sexual assault. With all the incidents happening around me, including my roommate's experience, I chose to focus on using art therapy in the recovery process for victims of rape. My roommate had already used her art as part of her healing, without any formal direction. She and her artwork became a major part of my thesis. I continued to take classes, carry a client caseload, and write my thesis.

By this time, my fiancé was in the police academy four hours away, so we were also trying to see each other many weekends. It was a lot to have taken on, and a lot to be going through. I am not sure if I ever accepted the fact that I actually had a choice in taking all of it on or continuing to do so. No one was forcing me, and I suppose quitting had always been an option. But perhaps it never felt like an option for me. Maybe because I felt like I had already lost so much. My life had already been upended the previous year. Maybe I put blinders on to all these traumatic events and decided to just push through.

So, after months of research, writing, and rewriting, my thesis was complete, and my supervisor suggested that I submit it to the American Journal of Art Therapy. It was accepted and published by the journal. This was a very proud moment, and at the end of it I felt a real sense of accomplishment. Not just for academic achievement, but for surviving the circumstances that went on during those eighteen months. Again, perhaps this was the first of many times I would refuse to give up. I had gotten through it.

I never went on to practice art therapy professionally for a number of reasons, but over the years, I have utilized my skills and training in a variety of ways and settings. I certainly always believed wholeheartedly in the healing powers of art, and the benefits it can offer everyone, but especially the victims of trauma. Most importantly, I have held it close and used it for myself hundreds of times for my own therapy, expression, and healing.

I went on to get a master's degree in human services counseling through a state college in a satellite office for the program, when my husband and I were first married. It was a great way to make the best of a time period when we lived in an area where there were not good options to have a job in my field; I could complete my education and meet some friends in the process.

We eventually were able to relocate closer to the area we were from and still had family. I worked briefly as a therapist before having children. I felt prepared for the therapist role but not at all seasoned for it, and there were some major issues within the agency that made me choose not to stay for long. During the time I was there, I met and helped some incredible people whom I have never forgotten. They were some of my first and most important clients.

While in the master's program, I had briefly considered going on for my doctorate. One professor strongly recommended it, feeling that I had what it took to follow that goal and achieve it. At that point, however, I couldn't see investing the time and money in that level of education, just to take a break to have children soon after completing it. I knew my husband would be working shift work his entire career, and I didn't want my future children to have a childhood that centered around daycare and crazy schedules. While I fully support that choice for all women, it wasn't the life I wanted, and I felt like I would never be doing justice to either role if I pursued both.

Any mom can tell you that being a mom is pretty good training for becoming a strong advocate, and that was certainly the case for me. You will never fight harder or better for anyone than your own child. It was important for me to raise my own kids, and I wouldn't trade it for anything. But I truly missed working and focusing on the skills that I was just beginning to develop. I am not good at doing things halfway, and never felt I could dedicate as much time to a career as I would want to while raising our boys. They deserved all my time and attention.

They grew up to be two of the most amazing people I know, and I am sure I made the right choice in those years. Those years raising them also challenged me in ways I had not imagined. But they also rewarded me in countless ways I could not have envisioned. These two young men are so exceptional in so many ways. They are as different as could be but are such a marvelous complement to each other.

So even after making the choice to not practice as a therapist, this topic and this work would call me back for many years after that, and in ways I would have never foreseen.

Chapter 29
Helping Friends Through Advocacy

Over the years, there were so many encounters with so many people—some I knew well and others I barely knew. Some who asked for help, others who shared their story with me. And yet others who simply became friends and never shared a story, but I always believed there was one. Hopefully just being there as a "safe" person would be enough for anyone who needed someone to talk to.

At some point after I left my job as an advocate, I realized that it had not left me. People who needed an advocate were just finding me in all kinds of ways. It wasn't always because of sexual or domestic violence (the advocacy my training was for), but often it was. I would like to think that my affinity and dedication to this work was so evident that people instinctively knew they would be safe coming to me. Or maybe I truly had a gift and fate had something to do with how I kept running into these people in various settings. And maybe it was totally random, but it sure didn't feel random. At one point, I even asked a few other of my friends if this happened to them—having people come into their lives who had had experiences with domestic or sexual violence, and your paths crossed and suddenly they were telling you their story. I got a lot of nos. So, I started to just accept it for what it was. Fate, coincidence, or just someone needing me.

At times, I truly needed a break from it. It was stressful to hear stories of people's terrible traumas every day. But I would never turn anyone away who needed someone, so I worked very hard at self-care. It is very easy to become so involved that you don't see the effect it is having on you. If it was a choice between continuing to help someone and needing to ramp up the ways I would take care of myself so I could continue to help that person, I would always choose taking care of myself so I could still help that person, listen, provide resources, whatever it was. There have only been a couple of instances where I have had to make another choice.

If you choose to advocate for others, you may find yourself in the situation of having to make difficult decisions in that delicate balance between taking care of others, but not at the expense of taking care of your own well-being. Secondary or vicarious trauma is still trauma, and you will feel the impact of dealing with it on a long-term or continual basis. You have to remember to take care of yourself first, or you will be in no condition to care for anyone else. You may have to make some tough choices such as taking a lesser role in a situation you have been very involved in, leaving a school, living or work environment where you have exposure to other people's trauma, or letting a friend know that you need a break. You may need to take time for yourself in other ways like cutting back hours at work or building in more time for some self-care and necessary breaks in emotionally demanding work.

If you can't control people exposing you to their difficult personal situations, you may need to take control over the amount of time that you are in that environment (if at all). At one point, I was having constant exposure to two such situations simultaneously: one in my personal environment where I had a lot of people leaning on me and turning to me for help, and the other in a work environment where a friend was going through a terrible situation personally. Neither source of emotional stress was changing (over a long period of time), so I finally had to make a tough decision and remove myself somewhat from both situations. I found that over a period of many months, it was just too demanding and draining. It wasn't fair to me, and I had to put on my own oxygen mask first or I would not have the ability to help anyone.

This will never be easy, as the people you truly want to help will still need you. But you may start to see the toll it is taking on you. For me, I couldn't get enough sleep. I was constantly exhausted even though I was sleeping far more than usual. Just when it seemed I couldn't possibly need more sleep, I did. I also felt like I was the one living through these situations, when in fact it was happening to other people. But I was hearing so much about them, it felt like they were happening to me. During this time, I was also getting far too many severe tension headaches, and it definitely correlated to the days I was hearing the most about the issues from these situations.

Again, with many other things I have described, no one will be able to draw this line or set this boundary but you. As a woman, if you find you need to do this, you may also need to fight the urge to apologize for it. We are socialized to take care of others, without regard for our own well-being. We do not have an endless supply of time and emotional energy. It is okay to acknowledge that. It doesn't make us weak or failures, it makes us human. Setting healthy boundaries yourself can be a good example for others.

Here are just a few examples of times people reached out for help or confided in me:

- A friend who called one day because they needed HIV testing and thought I would know where to take them

- A friend who told me about her parents' suicide and what it had done to her

- A co-worker who confided in me about her son's drug problem

- A friend who shared details of her son's serious illness

- A friend who was going through a terrible divorce and needed a little guidance to realize that the relationship had been abusive, and he was continuing that pattern during the divorce

- A friend who was going through a difficult breakup and needed help from someone to point out that he was stalking/abusing his partner by refusing to consent to the breakup

- A co-worker who faced possible criminal charges because of her child's actions

- A friend whose daughter had a life-threatening eating disorder and was in residential treatment for a year, during which time she had many setbacks and changes of treatment

- A friend who needed encouragement to file a restraining order against her former partner (We went together, and I continued to remind her why this was necessary.)

- A friend needing to find resources for her son, who had cancer twice

- A co-worker who was trapped in an unhealthy marriage and did not see any way out, and needed help seeing it was clearly abusive and a danger to her children as well as herself

- A co-worker and friend who had a life-threatening complication from surgery

- A co-worker whose partner was an alcoholic

- A friend who asked for help writing a letter to her estranged siblings

- A friend who told me about the sexual abuse of her friend that she witnessed as a teenager

- A friend who told me about her grandfather being a known pedophile

- A friend who leaned on me during her marital problems and long-term separation

- A family member whose daughter had to cancel her wedding at the last minute due to her fiancé being abusive

- A friend who confided in me about her long-term marital problems

- Preventing my friend's ex from entering her home to confront her when she would not answer his phone calls, and calling the police

- A pre-teen who came to me about a teenager who was experiencing domestic violence

- A young adult who confided in me about witnessing/ learning of several of his friends being sexually harassed, abused, and assaulted

- A friend who talked with me about her sister experiencing severe dementia and having difficulty coming to terms with it

- A friend dealing with her sibling's serious medical issues

- A friend asking for help coping with her physical disability

- An acquaintance confiding in me about her family member's sexual abuse as a child

- A co-worker confiding in me about his serious depression and struggle to stay on medication

- Helping a friend write a healing letter to her mother about being sexually abused as a child

- Helping a friend consider resources for her daughter with mental health issues and how to encourage her to face them

- Helping an acquaintance take the first steps to talk about being assaulted and then reach out for community resources and counseling

- Finding alternative counseling resources for a friend when their daughter's current provider was no longer an option

- Listening to a friend vent about her toxic family situation and then trying to problem-solve with her

This list certainly can sound like "normal" but difficult life circumstances and encounters with friends, and they are. But in each of these instances, advocacy skills and services can be applied to make each of these situations considerably better very quickly. Even when there are serious and difficult issues in front of you, there is always something that can be done to make it at least a little bit better right away. Chipping away at the list of things that must be done can make it less overwhelming.

While this is an extensive list of some very real problems, they can all be improved quickly with some direction and planning. Sometimes the person who is in the crisis is not able to see what those steps might be. A friend with advocacy skills can point out those steps to them. Looking back now, I realize that maybe I knew I was going to need all my strength for the situation that was coming next.

Chapter 30
When Those Meant to Advocate for Victims Betray Them

One day long after I had left the center for survivors, my phone started to blow up with messages from my former co-workers. I had left the agency in 2016, and it was August of 2022. The world had gotten through Covid, and maybe we were feeling like things would return to normal. Not so fast.

The mission of this agency was "to work to end domestic and sexual violence for all women, men and children." The agency served survivors of these crimes and when I worked there, they were all about doing everything to empower the survivor. The agency, in my opinion and that of many others, had experienced a downward slide in the quality of the services for the people it was serving, as well as a large shift from the original mission towards a focus on diversity above all else, including employee qualifications.

Things had been heading in this direction for at least the two years before I left, but I really didn't have an idea of the state of things by 2022. My husband and I had moved out of state, and I hadn't looked back at the agency, other than staying in touch with the friends who had been co-workers.

But on this day, I received three separate messages from former co-workers that the agency had hired a convicted sex offender in 2020 and he had been working at the agency since that time as a victim advocate. WHAT?! This had to be a mistake! The agency I knew would never have put victims at risk in that way. And what could have been the possible purpose of hiring him? What could they have been thinking?

This man would have had access to the client database, which meant he would have seen all the confidential client information including addresses, phone numbers, victim experiences, etc. He was obviously a huge risk of harming any of the clients or staff. This was going to be a nightmare. And when the story first broke, that was obvious. But as it unfolded, we would realize that it was even worse than the parts of the story that were revealed on the news.

One thing the agency hadn't counted on was the public outrage when the story broke, which of course eventually happened. But not only that, what about the nearly 100 former employees who had resigned and left the agency in record numbers as it had been becoming a shadow of its former self and failing to live up to its mission? After months to years of ignoring staff feedback, exit interviews with board members including the president, and employee attrition statistics that seemed too high to possibly be accurate, the agency would have to face us.

By the way, remember that those former employees were all skilled advocates. This would become a key factor in the protest movement that was about to ensue. I confess that when I first read the story, I still felt a distance from it. I was in another part of the country (and currently on vacation), hadn't worked there in many years, and didn't have a handle at all on what had been happening there. What could I possibly do about it now? Oh, what a loaded question that was.

Then I went on the website of the local news channel that had featured the story. I read that and then began to read the comments. Then I read a comment from a woman I didn't know named Emily. My brief exchange on Facebook with this woman pulled me into something that would consume me for the next eighteen to twenty-four months. And to this day, I can't thank her enough. She was the impetus behind me realizing that I had to get involved. Here is a copy of those original comments:

Emily: I think people can be reformed. But people in crisis if they had known? Would they be okay with this? Would they feel safe? I highly doubt it. It's a breach of trust between survivors and the organization whose whole purpose is to help.

Karen: So well said, thank you for your strength in articulating this so clearly. I worked at this agency for years, and I felt almost betrayed when I read this news today. I worked tirelessly during my time there to protect and make survivors feel safe and took great pride in that. As a volunteer coordinator there, I was tough when screening volunteers, because I didn't believe just anyone was appropriate to be with someone in such a vulnerable state. It feels as though that work is being invalidated by this. Sorry for the rant, I just wanted you to know that your thoughtful comments helped me.

Emily: Thank you for your work on behalf of survivors like myself. Honestly, I've spent way too much time on this post because it made me so angry for the victims out there knowing how this must feel for them. Your efforts weren't in vain if they kept up the standard on what was in your control. I just really hope that there is a shake-up in the mentality, otherwise there may need to be alternate group therapies, support groups, and so forth set up for victims who don't want their only choice to be an untrusted source.

Karen: Wow, thank you so much. This means so much to me, I will never question the quality of the work I did for victims, but sadly this is not the first time I've seen the work be "undone" or had measures I used to ensure the quality of service to victims removed at the agency after I left. Do you mind if I share your comment on my personal Facebook page? I'm still deciding if I want to share about this issue, but if I do, I would like to include your comments. I of course would only do that with your permission. Thank you again for your kind thoughts.

Emily: Feel free! Thank you again for your contribution to healing.

Karen: Thank you so much. It was the most valuable work I ever did, and it was truly an honor to help.

When I approached Emily later about getting her permission to include her and this exchange in this book, I explained what had transpired in my life since the fall-out mess from this agency's protest. She left me with these beautiful words: "When we are loud, it's because we know they are not in a position to be loud right now. And when someone hears, they know who the safe people are, even if they aren't ready to speak yet. Stay Loud."

So, after this exchange, even though we were on vacation at the time, it became obvious that this former group of employees needed to do what we knew how to do, advocate, and we needed to start now. We began to organize protest efforts. I don't think any of us realized how big it would become, but we were about to find out. I decided quickly that once I returned from vacation, I was probably going to have to fly to my home state for the protest.

We began to collect signatures for posters and letters of protest. We started a private group on Facebook for those of us who protested the agency's decision to hire this man. We organized an in-person protest, went to the agency a couple of different days, and invited the local news crew to attend. Our letters of protest eventually grew, and we realized that we needed to focus on two critical groups: survivors, and members of the community, including police, community therapists, medical, and other advocacy groups who had a vested interest in this field and this work. This community had a very active team of providers who responded to sexual assault calls routinely.

At the hospitals, there were specially trained nurses who were sexual assault nurse examiners to do the medical exams. There was an Abused Persons Unit division of the Sheriff's Department who were specially trained to question victims of sexual assault. Plus, another agency that specialized in responding to sexual abuse calls for children. This agency allowed everything but their initial medical exam to take place in one building to make it as easy as possible for the child. This included counseling, advocacy services, and all interactions with police.

My point in mentioning this is that this was not a community that had no services for survivors of sexual assault or an understanding of the complexities of this issue. And now the main agency, the one that had been the "gold standard" for those practices, had done the worst possible thing for victims and survivors.

We finally decided as a group that we needed to share our letters of protest with the media. Another friend and former co-worker who had been very active in the protest efforts and I decided to email the reporter covering the story. She immediately responded and wanted at least one of us to go on camera with the story and the letter. My friend was not comfortable being on camera, and I now lived out of state and had "nothing to lose" by speaking publicly and very vocally against an agency with such an impeccable reputation up until now. So it was decided very quickly that I would be interviewed.

I wish I could say I remember that first interview in great detail, but I don't. The whole period of time is a bit of a blur. I remember talking to a woman close to me, as my husband and I were boarding the plane. The interview was airing on the news the night we were flying into town and she had just watched it. We had taped it earlier that morning. All I can remember her saying was, "You could tell you were so angry." She quickly corrected herself that it wasn't in a bad way.

The next day when I watched the interview, I saw exactly what she had meant—you could feel my outrage, which under the circumstances felt very appropriate to me. I think it came through that I was outraged on behalf of all those victims and survivors who had been betrayed. That was exactly what needed to be conveyed, while remaining composed enough to convey it. I had done just that. From that moment on, I knew I would speak to the media any time it was necessary to keep this protest moving.

The group of people most severely affected by the agency's terrible decision was of course the victims and survivors themselves. Imagine that you are the survivor of sexual or domestic violence, and after a terrible period of time (or a lifetime) of being abused, assaulted, or mistreated … you finally get the courage to seek counseling or advocacy services. Now picture that you have a well-established relationship with a therapist or advocate, and suddenly you learn the news of this sex offender working at the agency. Again, picturing that he has access to everyone's private information, maybe you saw him in the office, or perhaps he was even your advocate in the office or at the hospital. Talk about being re-victimized!

This enormous group of people now had nowhere to go for services. Collectively, as a group of former employees, we were hearing from a lot of clients who now needed new therapists immediately. This agency was one of the only free places in the county that specialized in sexual assault and abuse. This was going to be a huge and long-term problem.

As a group, we spent a lot of time trying to connect people with the appropriate therapists, services, and practitioners. Through our Facebook group, we had a pretty efficient system for finding the right agency or therapist for each person. Those of us who were most active in the group were familiar with who was taking what types of clients and insurance, or we could quickly find out. We could also put a message out to the group and very quickly receive a response as to where to go next. Some of us joked that we were spending more hours on referrals now than we had when we worked at the agency.

The period when we were protesting what the agency had done to betray the people they served was full of activity. Protesting, collecting signatures, writing letters and a lot of time spent talking with each other online. Those of us who had sort of taken a leadership role were sharing information with each other multiple times a day, as we each had different contacts. It was hard to escape from, even when you knew you needed a break. We really didn't have the time to do that because everything was happening so quickly. The local news was on top of the story, and we needed our side of things to progress to the point of forcing the agency to make a public apology and have the key players hopefully resign as a show of accountability.

There was a lot of back-and-forth about the best way to achieve that. The fifty-plus people that included former employees and clients felt that the leadership had to completely change in hopes of any long-lasting change being implemented to begin to correct this wrong. Within a month, several of those resignations had happened, including the executive director we had all worked under.

Although I totally did not support what she had done by hiring this unqualified staffer, I also didn't believe that the director was the guiding force behind the decision to do so. Along with many others, I felt she had been scapegoated by the others involved to take the fall for this horrific decision. While it was still her responsibility to have prevented it (given that she was still the director), it was a terrible shame that after all her good work, this was what people would now remember.

VI.
Survivor Interviews, Part 3

Chapter 31
It All Led Up to This

When our protest group had begun gathering signatures for our survivor letter, I was overwhelmed by the response. The number of people who heard via Facebook or through their survivors' groups that we were collecting signatures was staggering.

Then one day, I got a random text from someone I knew very well. Michelle texted and just said, "Please add my signature to your survivor letter."

I was stunned and quickly responded, "Are you ok?" She answered, "Yes but I'm not ready to talk." I said, "Ok, I am always here" or something like that.

I did not know she was a survivor, and I was not sure how to process this new information. I kept the information to myself and truly hoped that she was all right. I just had to hope she would tell me more when she was ready.

At another point around that time, I believe we texted about something else, and I checked on her and asked if she was in therapy. She said she was, and we didn't talk more about it for a while.

The time was to come when that would change radically.

Chapter 32
Michelle

*Michelle's disclosure of abuse to me has changed so many things about the dynamics of all of her relationships, which of course is secondary to the major impact it had on her development, her ability to form relationships and trust others, as well as to heal from the abuse. What I would like to focus on here are the ways in which I have seen it change **her** for the better since she disclosed. This is someone I've known most of my life. Over the years, I definitely knew that she was unhappy. It was evident, and I didn't quite know why. But it was more than that, and now I know why. She never seemed confident or sure of herself, never very content or at peace. She didn't really stand up or speak up for herself. I **always** loved Michelle. But nothing could compare to how much I love this new version of her. She is free of the secret that imprisoned her for decades. And that confidence and ability to speak up for herself emerged in the most beautiful ways. I love seeing her at peace and with a contentment that I had never seen in her before. She is my **SHEro**. (Note: Michelle never worked with an advocate, because her sexual abuse was only recovered recently. She had repressed memories of it from childhood, and by the time she recalled the memories, it was unfortunately too late for her to pursue criminal charges against her abuser.)*

Michelle's Voice

Before I told anyone about the abuse, I felt truly alone. When the memories started to come back to me, they would be brief images or clips, not complete memories. When I finally disclosed it to someone I could trust, Karen completely believed me. While she was not my advocate, it was a role she had before and knew well. She pushed me to do things I wouldn't have been able to do on my own. But in a good way. I was glad that she was there to give me the push I needed. She was my voice when I could not be. She spoke for me until I was strong enough to speak for myself.

Once I had this support, for the first time in my life, I didn't feel crazy. I would have never gotten through this situation alone. Earlier in my life, my siblings were there with me. There are parts of my childhood that I am not sure I would have survived without them. Without the support since I disclosed the abuse to others, I do believe I would be hiding under a rock or in a psych ward.

As far as advice for someone who is just learning about a loved one being abused, I would say to prepare yourself because the information you will hear is difficult. Don't feel guilty about what you didn't know or didn't see. That is a tough one for most. Make sure she knows that she is loved and not alone. Give her a hug (with permission) so she can feel your support.

The reaction of the first person that you tell is important because it affects how you feel about yourself, your experience and your ability/willingness to tell anyone else. Each person that I told, when it went well, it gave me strength and confidence to continue sharing my story. What I wish other survivors knew (those who haven't disclosed), is that telling people starts to get rid of the shame you've been holding all those years. It was never ours to hold in the first place, and now you will begin to feel and believe that.

As far as obstacles to my telling people sooner, the biggest was definitely that I didn't think people would believe me, because of who he was. I second-guessed myself a lot. That continued until a time when someone close to me shared a similar experience. That again made me feel more confident in my ability to share my own experience.

I definitely had embarrassment about my situation and felt gross any time I had to be around him. I think I felt that way because I had allowed him to manipulate me. I am slowly accepting the fact that I had no ownership of the situation because I was a child. It wasn't up to me to protect myself from him or anticipate that he might try to hurt or manipulate me. I was conditioned and manipulated into believing that the abuse was not wrong. That shame is all his.

When I first recalled what had happened to me, I knew I could not tell my father. Because I was afraid of his reaction. The things that would have been huge setbacks to me a year ago are not as major as they were. At one time, I would have panicked and felt like I couldn't breathe. I have more coping skills now, and those same setbacks do not bring me to rock-bottom anymore.

Going to therapy has made a major difference. I am talking to the people I trust the most. I am an open book now. I no longer have to hide anything from anyone. I have let go of those who don't believe or support me. They are no longer in my life.

I want the people reading this book to be reminded that they never know what someone else is going through. They can't know and shouldn't judge. I would encourage them to listen.

The reason I hesitated to tell some people was that they believed the previous lies and stories told about me. I felt as though I had ruined our family. I felt like I had been the biggest disappointment. Some people went out of their way to tell me as much. But once this huge secret was finally out, I was free to be myself. I could breathe and relax, and not worry about hiding anything. The right people now believed me, and that made a difference.

For many years, my voice was silenced. I was living with a secret that became so crippling I became an entirely different person. I hid behind walls so tall no one was allowed in. That is until Karen posted on Facebook what would become the beginning of my peace. She was in the process of finding survivors to sign a petition, I took this as a sign I needed to open up, even if just slightly, and asked her to add me to the survivor list. This was the smallest step, but for me the biggest step I had ever taken on this subject.

Months later, I happened to be in the same location as Karen. In walked my abuser …

Karen's calming presence, her caring heart, her trusting and safe smile were exactly what I needed to finally share my full secret. With a heart racing so strong and anxiety that was bubbling up to my throat, I finally let out the words, "I was sexually abused, and it was him." This was something I had been holding in for over three decades.

Over the next several months, things would be terrifying for me. Telling my secret to my entire family was harder than expected. The lack of support, being told I was a liar, a family member tarnishing my name, and being bullied was something no one should ever have to live through. Every step of this healing process has been a struggle. Karen's knowledge in this area and guidance every step of the way was what I lacked all these years. I truly believe if it weren't for my voice being empowered by the advocate I had in Karen, this secret would have stayed buried until the day I was laid to rest.

Chapter 33
Everything Has Changed

When Michelle told me who her abuser was, the shock was almost more than I could process. It took months for it to begin to sink in. In some ways, even though it has been over a year, I still don't think it has truly sunk in. In many ways, that day changed everything about how I viewed the world. Many of the things I had always believed in had been a lie, and I was facing coming to terms with this also.

So many of my memories were all tainted, dirty, and vile. Had anyone else known or suspected? Certainly, there must have been red flags. And there were people I would never trust again. If they could lie about this, I truly would have no use for them to be in my life. My husband and I had been the only ones entrusted with this information (for now), and we would be in a position for months of being unable to share it with others close to us.

During the process of trying to make sense of all this, many flashes of memories kept flooding back into my mind. Memories that now had a much different meaning. Memories of things that now seemed wildly inappropriate, in the context of knowing there was abuse happening in that house. There were at least five different memories that I had, some that there were even photos of, that now have completely different meanings. They are the missing puzzle pieces that kept me (and others) from putting this evil puzzle together so long ago, at a time when it might have prevented so much of the pain it had caused.

Sometimes things can seem like an innocent accident, or just something that "this family does differently", when in fact they are indicators of something truly wrong happening right under your nose. Trusted adults get away with it because people are willing to overlook those things in hopes that all is normal and will remain as such. Michelle's abuser had been portraying himself as kind, "normal" and reputable for decades, with the type of career that made him seem like an authority, while simultaneously depicting his victim as crazy, mentally ill, and unstable. Well played, you sick *fuck*.

Chapter 34
Trying to Understand the Impact of Child Sexual Abuse

Many people don't have a clear understanding of why childhood sexual abuse changes a person's entire life the way that it does. I think it is difficult to understand if you haven't experienced it, and I know I can't truly grasp it. But I will try to explain it to the best of my limited ability. I myself had only one small incident as a pre-teen with an extended family member that helps me to understand it somewhat. We were staying with a family member. I was about twelve or thirteen, and we were all sleeping downstairs in the basement on the floor. During the night I awoke to him grabbing my breast.

To this day, I don't know if this was "an accident" because he was next to his wife on the other side of me, and he was obviously used to being in bed with her. Maybe he actually did this in his sleep. A stretch, I know, but I attempted to give him the benefit of the doubt. And I doubt very much that my breast, at that age, felt like the breast of a grown woman. So wouldn't that have made him wake up and realize if it truly were a mistake?

Yet my entire life, I have failed to characterize this as sexual abuse because on the larger scale of things, it was so minor compared to what most victims experience. And the fact that I never confronted him or found out if it was intentional didn't help. If I had, maybe I would feel confident in labeling it. But most importantly, maybe it gives me a small bit of understanding that others with no experience like this may not have.

Again, I have never wanted to compare this to the situations of those who have experienced long-lasting and invasive sexual abuse, and I don't. This was nothing like that. It was, luckily, a few brief moments out of my young life that fortunately were over quickly. But it did give me a tiny glimpse into what that type of behavior does to a person. Prior to that experience, I had no reason not to trust all the adults in my life. I had been lucky so far and had really only had encounters with decent people—especially family members—whether they were close relatives, family friends, or (like this person) out-of-town relatives who I rarely saw.

In that moment, I learned that I could not necessarily trust adults. That was a hard lesson to learn, and one I had not expected. I literally learned and internalized that lesson overnight. Even the ones who were "family" could or would hurt me if given the opportunity or motivation. I also learned in that moment that it was up to me, and only me, to protect myself or advocate for myself. Looking back at it now, I believe that this is also a large part of where my strong belief to stand by someone who needs you began.

Chapter 35
Mary Lee

I want to share my special connection with Mary Lee. We volunteered together years ago at our local Rape Crisis Center. She trained me as a new volunteer advocate. She was incredibly knowledgeable and compassionate and was a valuable mentor. But years after we met, I learned that she also knew my dad from the grocery store he owned and ran in another nearby community. As I interviewed Mary Lee (decades after Dad had passed away), I took comfort in being reminded that they knew each other. He cashed her paychecks for her every week at that small-town grocery store for over five years, as it was on the way to an evening teaching job she held for thirty-five years. Mary Lee's stories of survival surprised me as I had not known them prior to writing this book, yet in another way, they did not. I think it would be unusual for someone to have her level of empathy, compassion, and insight without having experienced this kind of pain herself. Thank you, Mary Lee, for sharing your courageous story with us.

Mary Lee's Voice

I experienced two rapes in my lifetime. One was when I was around ten. It happened with someone from our community. My mother said, "Don't you dare say anything—it will ruin our reputation in the neighborhood." The second time, I was a senior in college, and it was the night before graduation. A bunch of us were out, and I was attacked by another student. We graduated the next morning, and after that, I went to Europe for a month. It was 1962.

Years later, a friend encouraged me to apply to volunteer at the local Rape Crisis Center as a victim advocate. It was these early experiences in my life that I believe made me so effective in that role. I was natural, and I was helping others deal with the pain I had faced.

In my opinion, advocacy should begin at about age two. If we learned what advocacy meant from a young age, we would make better decisions, we would be educated, we would be educated and would know what our options are. If I had had that information, all of my choices would have been different in both situations of assault in my lifetime. Without advocacy, we don't even know what the resources are, much less being able to access them. It would allow families to have a safe way to talk about abuse when it does occur.

If I knew someone who was going to come forward to disclose abuse to a family member, I would encourage them "to surround themselves with people who support you." You are on a new journey, and that journey needs to be one of acceptance. Don't ever let anyone tell you to "get over it, it is in the past." "Forgive and forget" is another very popular, harmful, and inaccurate statement that people make that is not helpful.

If the first person I talked to about my rapes had had a negative reaction, it would have caused me to regress and hide away again in shame and guilt. Things could have continued that way until someone came forward to help me. I feared people's rejection, I was afraid of how it would affect my career and standing in the community. Survivors need to have hope, and they need to have a reason to hope.

I felt shame and embarrassment about my situation because we are taught that at an early age. "You caused it." You can't easily go to your mom and dad because of the guilt associated with it. I couldn't tell my mom because of what she had said the first time I was raped as a child. I knew it would be more of the same, and I just couldn't face that again. Years after my college assault, I found the strength to tell my father. He told me he just wanted to support me now, and that if he had known back then, he probably would have killed the guy. I never told my mom because I could still feel her judgment from the first rape decades later.

I felt the same judgment and rejection that I had always experienced from my mother. Since I had had therapy and advocacy, I am in a much better place to help others, and that happens a lot. People reach out to me frequently with their own situations, and I want to be able to help them. People seek me out because they somehow sense that I am a safe and open person to come to. This has happened to me numerous times throughout my life.

I want the people reading this book to know that advocacy groups need to advocate with physicians' offices. They need to educate doctors, nurses, and staff to be able to offer hope and help immediately. If someone was there to educate these professionals, they would be able to offer intervention and help immediately when identifying an abusive situation. In my situation, I felt judged and unsafe to tell people because I had witnessed them being judgmental about other things. And I knew this attitude would transfer to other issues such as my rapes. Be aware of how you present yourself to the world. It matters and impacts how approachable you are to others.

If families and schools were educated, and skilled enough to know how to talk to a mother so that she is able to help her child when a child discloses abuse, that could help the child, and eventually bridge that gap that exists between a child in pain and the services that are available. They are only "available" when someone knows how to access them.

Chapter 36
What to Expect from a Disclosure of Sexual Abuse or Assault

There are a few facts about domestic and sexual abuse that I will share here, along with some things that happen when a survivor discloses that it has happened to her:

- Many of your friends and family may have no prior knowledge of domestic or sexual violence prior to you reaching out to them. This is not something everyone has encountered. You should know this before taking too much of their advice to heart. They may mean well but have absolutely no basis in fact for their opinions and beliefs. I have heard from friends many false beliefs such as, "Well, he has never hurt you before, so you have no reason to believe he will do so now." And "I've never had any reason to doubt his credibility or think he is capable of something like this."

- It is uncommon for there to be only one victim of a particular pedophile. This is a sickness that typically needs to find an outlet, and tragically, it usually does.

- One member of a family is often scapegoated and made to feel like the problems in the family come from them. That person being the one to tell the family about the problem does not make them the source of the problem. Just because the major issues raised were not out in the open before the survivor came forward does not mean they were caused by that person. Imagine blaming the victim of any other crime for them having been victimized (robbery)!

- It is common for lies to be perpetuated within the family to support the story that allows the abuse to continue.

- Don't ever assume "he has never hurt me before" means that he will not hurt you now. Especially if he is experiencing a loss of control over you for the first time.

- You will really find out who truly believes and supports you during this process, and it may not be who you think or expected.

- You may need to make some tough decisions about who doesn't get to come with you on the rest of your journey, and it may be so hard, or it may be the easiest choice you've ever made.

- People who had pledged their support of you may withdraw it once it hits too close to home or starts to get really ugly. Stay strong; you are still doing what is right for you.

- The truth always wins over the lies, even if not everyone knows it, or believes what you know to be true. You know it, and sometimes that has to be enough, at least for now.

- Do not underestimate the lengths an abusive person will go to maintain control of you, the situation, or the narrative that everyone is hearing about that person and you.

- Don't fall into the trap of falling into the belief system of the lies that are being told about you. Just because an abusive person tells them and someone believes them does not make them any more true.

- You may find yourself in the position of standing up for one person and knowing you will lose a lot of others in the process. You know what is right; do that no matter what.

- Many women stand behind their abusive partner/husband, even when faced with the hard truth that that person is a pedophile. Some people need to believe that it isn't true and will overlook all sorts of evidence to make it so. It will feel like this is about you, but it is about them. You may need to walk away from them, and that is okay.

- Some people will require "proof" in order to believe you. These are not your people. Keep people close who truly believe you without conditions. They won't require proof or verification of your story from others. The fact that you are saying it will be enough. You are enough.

- It is excruciating to tell your whole family about being victimized by one of the people who was responsible for caring for and protecting you, and someone you should have been able to trust. And it is even more difficult if this is a person they are still close to.

- You may be called a liar, unreliable, dramatic, mentally ill, or anything that supports the theory that you are the problem.

- Even losing a lot of the people you have always been close to is not as bad as living behind the crippling secret you have been living with.

VII.
Advocacy

Chapter 37
Types of Settings Where Advocacy is Often Needed

In several of the settings listed below, I have had extensive experience, and the length of that section reflects my experiences. Other sections include a brief commentary, because I have worked less directly in those fields. The brevity of those sections is not reflective of the only ways advocacy can be used in those settings, but I am writing based on my own experience and referring you to general resources.

Medical & within the school setting:

There are countless examples of when medical advocacy can be needed—for example, in advocating for your own medical care, that of your child, that of an aging parent. A parent of a child with a medical condition is often immediately thrown into the role of medical advocate on behalf of their child. This happens without warning, and almost always without any expertise on the medical condition their child was just diagnosed with. This can happen on a small scale with minor illnesses or injuries that are not immediately diagnosed. You may need to seek a second opinion or specialist and may have to advocate to get it.

Many times, parents have more awareness and knowledge of their child's health, which is more extensive than doctors would like to admit. Their parental instincts, added to that, can put them in a better place than the doctor to know what might be needed next. This is not usually a popular experience with doctors and nurses, as they are used to having expertise in medical situations. While they are the medical experts, as the parent you are the expert on your child. You know best when something doesn't seem right. You may have to be unpopular or nag a little bit to get the care for your child that you feel is required.

With more serious conditions, this is obviously even more essential and a much more long-term process and role for the parent. If your child has a life-threatening illness like cancer, or a life-changing and potentially life-threatening illness like a serious peanut allergy or type 1 diabetes, you will be thrust into the situation of needing to learn an absolute ton of medical information, whether you have an affinity for this type of information or not. You now have no choice; your child's life depends on it.

There is no room for a learning curve. Your education, the test on what you've learned, and putting it to immediate use will all happen on the same day. You most often take your child home and need to know how to keep them safe, the same day after you have just learned how to do so. This is terrifying to say the very least. It is a role you have just assumed for a long period of time, perhaps indefinitely. You will now be overseeing your child's medical care. Then you will be figuring out how to assist them in the school environment while recovering from or coping with an ongoing medical issue. You will have to put dozens of things in place to keep them physically safe in school, a way to see that these protocols are implemented and followed, and a plan for if and when they are not.

You will most likely need to develop a 504 plan or an Individualized Education Program (IEP). A 504 plan protects students with disabilities and describes the accommodations that the school will provide to support the child's education. These plans provide civil rights protection to all individuals with disabilities in programs that received federal funding, which includes public schools. In the case of a child with special medical needs, the 504 will include things that allow the child a safe environment that doesn't interfere with the quality of their education. For example, a child with a peanut allergy will be in a classroom where precautions are taken where no peanuts or peanut products are brought into that classroom so as to not to endanger that child. A child with type 1 diabetes will be allowed to test their blood sugar right at their desk, rather than reporting to the nurse's office, losing up to a half-hour or more of class time each day. A 504 plan is a blueprint for how the school will support a student with a disability and remove any barriers to learning. The goal is to give the student equal access to school in the least restrictive environment possible.

An IEP is a legal document under United States law that is developed for each public-school child in the U.S. who needs special education. It is created through a team of the child's parents and district personnel who are knowledgeable about the child's needs. It describes the plan for the student's educational program, including current performance levels, student goals, and the educational placement and other services the student will receive. The IEP process is complex, but it is also an effective way to address how your child learns. An IEP is a legal document that clearly defines how a school plans to meet a child's unique educational needs that result from a disability.

The development of a 504 or an IEP both involve an enormous amount of learning on the part of the parents in order to complete the process, and an enormous amount of advocacy, as you learn and then make clear to others, what your child will require to learn in a safe environment with the fewest limits placed on the child while they learn.

Another huge aspect of raising a child with a medical condition is the aspect of how you manage things like playdates and birthday parties. This takes some advocacy of a different type. You need to make sure that your child is physically safe but can also participate in all these normal parts of childhood without feeling "different" from the other kids. This can be an impossible task, but as a parent you will do your absolute best to make both of those things simultaneously possible—or as close as it can be.

There are a lot of great support groups to help you to meet other parents who have navigated the same challenges. You can gain ideas and support from each other while trying to meet others who understand the situations you are facing with your child and attempting to keep their life as normal as possible.

Chapter 38
Workplace Advocacy

There are, of course, many ways you will often use advocacy in relation to your work environment. You may need to advocate for better or fair working conditions or pay. You may face discrimination in one form or another because of your gender, race, gender identity, or physical limitations or challenges. In all of these situations, you will need to advocate for yourself to improve your work circumstances.

A clear expectation that you expect and demand to be treated fairly is often a good start. It does not need to be confrontational. Depending on the situation, you can simply state something like one of the following:

- "I believe it is against the law to ask me in a job interview when I plan to have children."

- "I am sure you realize that you are paying me far less money for the same job that my male co-worker is doing and earning a better salary."

- "It is against the law to discriminate against a person for their gender identity. If I am qualified to do the job and am doing so well, that is the only thing that is relevant."

- "I am entitled to report being sexually harassed in the workplace and have an expectation to be able to work in a non-hostile environment."

Know your rights in each of the above examples, and any others you may encounter. Then take the necessary steps to ensure that your rights are being met and respected. Refer back to the description earlier in this chapter about the most important skills involved in advocacy. Each will be used in each of these situations and many others.

Be organized, make a list of what you need to do, but break it into small manageable steps and do your research on ways to solve your problem. Work through your list a little bit at a time. The fact that you are so well prepared will let your boss or human resources department know that you are serious and will not have your concerns dismissed without being addressed in a real way.

I believe most of us have experienced situations at work that would fall into the categories of bullying or harassment. There are usually no checks and balances in place to ensure that this never happens. Most workplaces rely heavily on the personal relationships between co-workers, and it would be impossible that there would never be issues when personalities are involved. Most women have also experienced sexism in the workplace. And the combination of sexism and bullying or harassment is not a pleasant one, or one that is uncommon.

In one of my jobs, I was required to supervise a project that raised money for the two non-profit agencies who participated in it. I represented the agency I worked at, and the other agency hired an employee's husband to work part-time for them, just to run this annual project. He was a sexist, and an overall miserable person. He didn't really know what it meant to compromise, listen to someone else's opinion, or work with someone. And his not being a regular employee of the agency was not helpful in relation to the issues he was causing for me. The things he said to me were way over the line of what was reasonable.

He wouldn't work with anyone or even talk about options of how to do things that weren't his idea. He instead barked orders as if I was his subordinate (or as though he was in any sort of supervisory position and had authority over me, which he did not), would berate every idea I attempted to share, was as condescending as possible at all times, and often raised his voice to the point of yelling.

One day we were on the phone, and he was in a particularly foul mood, and things were escalating. He got louder and more belligerent, and all I could think about was that this was never going to change unless I made it clear that it needed to. I had to set a clear boundary with him, or I wasn't going to be able to do my job. So when he finally stopped talking/yelling, I told him that we were going to be doing things differently. I reminded him that I worked at an agency whose mission was to end abuse in all forms, and his behavior was abusive.

I told him if he ever spoke to me in the way he had been, or raised his voice to me again, I would be contacting his employer to report his inappropriate behavior. I would also notify my boss that I would refuse to work with him because he was creating a hostile environment, leaving both agencies in a precarious position to be able to continue with this major fundraiser. I told him that going forward, if he spoke to me this way on the phone, I was simply going to hang up. This was the end of the majority of our issues dealing with each other. He was still unpleasant and difficult, but we communicated only when necessary and he never raised his voice to me again.

Chapter 39
Other Settings Where Advocacy Is Valuable

There are numerous other settings and situations in which advocacy is greatly needed. This chapter describes nine of these settings. It is important that what you gain from reading this section is the knowledge and confidence that the tools of advocacy can improve any situation, no matter how difficult. It can't make everything okay again, but it can get you moving in the right direction, and you will be able to take some control over a situation that likely has you feeling out of control and helpless.

Mental Health Care

Any time you have to face the medical/mental health system, it can be very overwhelming. It is a complex and detailed system, and people trying to navigate within it often experience many obstacles and roadblocks. Seeking mental health services has to be one of the most complicated processes and systems. Many times, if there is a mental health issue, it may be new or foreign to the person affected. It may have been precipitated by a traumatic event, and the symptoms the person is experiencing may be totally unfamiliar, as they have never encountered them before. Learning about the resources available will likely take a good amount of research. Don't be afraid to reach out to others for more information and resources.

These challenges are made more complicated by the enormous stigma our society still has surrounding anything to do with mental health. While we have made great strides, it is far from being seen on an even playing field with physical health. When you are advocating on behalf of a family member, a crucial first step is for you to attempt to remove this stigma as a barrier to your loved one receiving mental health care. You can do this by showing them that their issue is a medical problem, and it needs treatment like any other medical problem. Your attitude of there being no need to be ashamed or embarrassed will be a great first step in their accepting this to be true for themselves also. Hopefully over time, they will adopt your positive and open-minded attitude, and begin to internalize it as their own.

Again, the steps and skills about advocacy are applicable here as well.

If you search mental health resources on the Internet, you will be directed towards agencies in your local area.

Chemical Dependency

Many times, a person in crisis with alcohol or chemical dependency will need assistance from someone who can serve as an advocate for them. They are typically not thinking clearly and cannot act in their own best interests. They need someone to help with decisions about treatment, medical options, and financial decisions. Advocacy is important so that the individual always has a voice in decisions about their life and has the information about all options available to them. The individual needs to be empowered to exercise their rights and able to challenge health and social care professionals. (Repper & Perkins, 2003; Shepherd, Boardman and Slade, 2008)

Peer advocacy is also often used to support those in recovery as peers can share their experiences, successes, and failures, while making sure the individual is making the most of the opportunities and enabling them to combat anxieties about moving forward. Peer supporters may also provide a listening ear and mentoring about recovery, supporting the person through transitions between and after assistance services. (*imroc.org*)

Personal Relationships

The skills and steps mentioned above and in the definition section of this chapter are all incredibly helpful in navigating the most difficult situations in your personal relationships. Clear communication and being assertive about your own needs will go very far toward improving every relationship you are in. While brutal honesty can be very difficult to achieve and maintain, it goes a long way to help avoid the countless misunderstandings and disagreements that will be caused by not clearly communicating your needs, expectations, and disappointments.

Domestic or Sexual Violence

Check with your local domestic violence agency for the resources in your area. If you are not familiar with this local resource, an Internet search for it is a great place to start. Most of these agencies have trained advocates who can work with you on the specific issues related to domestic violence (DV) and sexual assault (SA).

Once assigned an advocate, that person will help you to navigate the various systems you will need to as you go through the process of leaving an abusive marriage or relationship. They can help you navigate the court system and legal system, and help you fill out an order of protection. They will help you find a place to stay temporarily, and get info on the local shelter, support groups, and low-cost housing options if necessary.

Legal

A legal advocate can help in many ways as you need to gain information on the legal system when you must navigate through it. Depending on the issues you are experiencing, there may be one or more forms of advocacy at your disposal. Do an online search for legal advocacy to find more of what you are looking for.

A legal advocate can let a client know their rights in each area that they may encounter. The advocate can help someone be made aware of all their legal options, as well as the best way for them to stay safe while navigating the legal system in the context of their particular situation, whether they are a victim of domestic violence, are seeking custody of their child, or going through a divorce. Chances are, the legal system is not familiar to the individual unless they have relied on it before, so during a very stressful time, they will be trying to take in massive amounts of information about a very complex system.

Criminal Justice System

You can begin with your local police station or sheriff's department itself to find information. Many have professional advocates on staff to assist victims of crime. Being the victim of a crime can be traumatic. A victim advocate can work with individuals to reduce the effects of trauma. The advocate will also be a key factor in getting them connected with organizations that provide important services like counseling. There also may be services provided by your state that are free of charge for the victims of crime. Check out government websites and use your internet search to find more information.

LGBTQ Community

Look to others in this community who can lead you in the right direction to get more information about services and resources that will be helpful. There are a number of large organizations throughout the country focusing on the specific rights and needs of the LGBTQ+ community. Again, a quick Internet search will lead you to these organizations in your area and around the country. They have a focus on advocacy, activism, and a policy agenda that focuses on creating inclusive policies and protections for the members of this community. They also include policy analysis, forums and enforcement efforts covering the issues that most impact the LGBTQ+ community. (The Center: The Lesbian, Gay, Bisexual & Transgender Community Center New York, New York, February 16, 2024)

Others in this community are your best resource. They have already been through a lot of what you might be looking for already. They probably know of places that are supportive of the unique issues in this community of people and the issues and bigotry they face. There are many resources online to help with support, such as the Trevor Project and the Human Rights Campaign.

Issues Related to Aging and Senior Living

Many communities have very active senior centers and other resources for seniors. Do an online search for information and centers like this, as well as putting a post on social media to find out what resources are available from other people you know. Search for other spots where this information may be found like church bulletins, local libraries, bookstores, and any place where community events are held.

AARP is a nonprofit membership organization dedicated to addressing the needs and interests of people fifty and older. Their site provides useful information and resources on topics such as health and wellness; economic security and work; long-term care and independent living; and personal enrichment. The National Council on Aging is also an amazing resource. There are local resources specific to your state to check out as well.

Each of these resources can provide ways for you to advocate for your own needs, or the needs of your loved one as they experience the transitions and challenges of aging. Just making yourself aware of what is available is a great way to advocate for yourself.

Physical or Mental Disabilities

Of course, people with physical or mental disabilities often need advocacy in many areas of their lives, and many times may have someone working with them in this capacity. Without someone working on their behalf, they will not have their physical, mental, or emotional needs met. It is completely unfair that so many people don't receive the help that they need, simply because they don't have an advocate or someone close to them advocating for them. There are a number of resources in this area as well. Websites to look at include The Arc, disability rights organizations, *HHS.gov,* and many more.

Chapter 40
My Medical Self-Advocacy

Twice in my life I have had significant injuries that were not solved easily with one of the first methods prescribed to treat them. When I was in my early twenties, I sprained my ankle exercising, and it would simply not heal, even with physical therapy and repeated attempts from multiple therapists trying every form of treatment they had in their arsenal. This went on for over a year, and I continued to go back to my family doctor asking, "What else can we try? This isn't working."

By this point, I wasn't only experiencing sharp pain, by now I also had poor circulation in the foot below the ankle and it would become extremely cold and turn blue or purple. This could not possibly be good. I was not getting very far, but eventually they referred me to an orthopedist, and he wanted to do exploratory surgery to "see what we find." Nope! I went back to my family doctor as we got closer to approaching two years, and his brilliant statement was, "You know, sometimes my ankles hurt too." Really?! "Are yours also forty-five degrees to the touch and purple?" Time for a new family doctor also.

By this time, my physical therapist and I were very close. She had worked tirelessly to help me for almost a year, and I did not fault her in any way for not curing me. She recommended that I see her husband, who was a massage therapist. She really felt that circulation was a major issue at this point. It was an excellent idea, and it wasn't too long into treatment before I saw minor improvements, and then more significant ones. Maybe we were finally onto something!

The therapists finally diagnosed me with reflex sympathetic dystrophy, a condition that is quite rare and usually only found in athletes. Eventually it was totally cured; it was amazing. After two years, I was finally feeling normal again. This was my introduction to the amazing things that were possible with massage therapy. I was a believer, and I would need to look to massage therapy again later in life.

In the year 2000, I was involved in a major car accident and would go on to experience very significant health complications as a result. Like most things I do, my particular complications were not simple or easy to diagnose and treat. It involved a period of years persisting in a variety of forms of medical care, treatment, specialists, complicated procedures, medications, and a ton of frustration, feeling I would never be healthy again. I was thirty years old with two young children.

Here is a partial list of the treatment I sought out in approximate order. I honestly did not keep a record and should have.

- Physical therapy for a period of months following the accident and then another attempt months to years later

- Chiropractic care began following the accident in 2000 and has continued since then. In twenty-four years, I saw a total of six or seven different chiropractors, including a period of four to five months where I tried an intensive form of adjustment three times a week.

- Massage therapy began a year or so after the accident. I have seen a total of ten to twelve massage therapists for varying lengths of time (a minimum of several months each). The one I continue to see (even though I now live in another state) has become my "primary care consultant" for everything medical, and a close friend and confidant to this day.

- I tried a variety of exercises and stretching like yoga, most of which made it worse.

- I saw an arthritis doctor who wanted to immediately diagnose me with rheumatoid arthritis. This made no sense as my issue was localized to the area affected by the accident and only on one side of the body. Each medical professional was convinced that their specialty would be the one to cure me, most with no evidence to support why.

- Then came acupuncture. This was a little out there for me, but it seemed possible, and I was open to it. I loved the doctor, and for a short time it helped. But the same thing happened as with many other therapies that I tried. After a few weeks, it would seem to be working, but after a couple of months, it was like the novelty had worn off.

I came to believe that my body responded to the shock to my system caused by introducing a new therapy or practitioner, and then once it became acclimated to it, it had no healing effect at all.

- I saw a couple of different pain doctors and started out with their easier procedures first like cortisone injections, another type that I don't remember, and eventually a procedure called radiofrequency.

No one in the medical community seemed to care that my quality of life was terrible, and I was in constant pain. This was a shock to me, I guess I was naïve enough to expect them to get to the bottom of it, or at least to care that they couldn't. Each specialist just wanted to give me pills and insisted that their specialty was the way to go. In a short period of time, my body would prove them to be wrong. I went to a pain management specialist and was recommended to try some very invasive procedures with one of their doctors. I eventually agreed to try.

The worst of these was radiofrequency, which uses heat to destroy the tissue by sending radio waves through a precisely placed needle to heat an area of the nerve. This then prevents pain signals from being sent back to the brain. In my case, my problems originated from the neck, so that was where the needle was. So the large needle is inserted and then the heat comes to zap the nerve. It is not a short process each time they do it. If this sounds torturous, I promise you that it is. To add to the horrible experience, radiofrequency could only be performed by one of the doctors at the pain clinic.

This doctor had no compassion or personality. I think it is fair to describe her as "charm-free." Even as I was wincing on the table in pain during the procedure, almost in tears and struggling to hold still, she never showed one word or gesture of comfort or concern. She was a robot, which only added to the feeling I was being tortured. What made it worse was that the procedure did not work, and caused some significant side effects that went on for months after the procedure. I was having zings of pain that would shoot through my head in an unpredictable way. My doctor's office had little to offer me other than to tell me repeatedly that my side effects were "not normal," and there was nothing that could be done. I believed these effects to be from the procedure, but after two months of hearing that it wasn't a normal side effect of the procedure, I began to wonder if I was also developing a brain tumor.

This same medical office put me on a fairly addictive medication that I was led to believe to be totally harmless for a period of years. I continued to express my concerns to my doctor at each visit about remaining on the medication with little to no improvement in my pain from taking it. After a period of time, I told the doctor I wanted to go off the medication, and she agreed I could do so. I experienced some strange feelings and emotions in the weeks after I went off the medication. I later learned that it was very important to wean myself off this med slowly. I had specifically asked my doctor this question and had been told no, just stop taking it. One of the possible results of coming off it too quickly was suicidal thoughts and actions. That was the end of me seeing this pain management practice. They had shown so little concern for my health and well-being, most notably in the way she had me just stop taking the medication abruptly. I could no longer adopt a "doctor knows best" philosophy with this practice, so I stopped seeing them.

One thing I will never regret is that I resisted several attempts from pain doctors to prescribe addictive narcotics and opioids. As much pain as I was in, I knew that my pain was not going to end because it could not be fixed or cured, so if I took a drug, I would most likely need to stay on it indefinitely. If I became addicted to it, I would then have another huge problem on my hands to add to my first issue. I knew that a life on narcotics could not possibly be the answer. On my darkest days now, when I have a crippling migraine or cannot move my neck without sharp pain, I try to remind myself of that. It could have been made even worse.

And of course, I also try to be grateful that I wasn't killed or paralyzed in the accident, which certainly could have happened. But when you experience chronic pain, it is very hard to hold onto that thought on a daily basis. I have been living with this pain for almost twenty-five years now and am still only in my mid-fifties. This is not easy, and it is not easy to look at the many years I hopefully have yet to live, and to wonder how I will manage the pain as my spine and discs continue to get worse.

My point in telling these stories is two-fold. One is to let people know that they are not alone in their frustration or inability to get quality answers or medical care for their issues. So many people experience this level of frustration in not being able to find adequate answers to their health challenges, or acceptable solutions to manage their pain. The other is to remind them that if you don't advocate for yourself, no one will. This is especially true if you are having an issue that is not being overseen by your family doctor.

Following my accident, I was responsible for seeking out the long list of medical professionals I previously listed. My family doctor had originally referred me for physical therapy and chiropractic care, and eventually an MRI when things weren't improving. When those had been completed-and weren't working, I wasn't given other options or suggestions. I began to go outside the area of conventional medicine and therapies.

Then one day someone gave me the name of a cranial sacral massage therapist. I didn't know what that meant, but my friend couldn't stop raving about her, so I called to make an appointment. When we met, I immediately liked the therapist, Lauren Felice, personally, but that didn't mean she could heal me. I had been down this road many times before. I wasn't about to get my hopes up after years of the same old thing with each new specialist. But a few weeks in, I had a feeling she might finally be different. She was incredibly intuitive and somehow could read my body and know what it needed before I told her, and many times when I had no idea what it needed myself.

Again, she didn't convince me right away, but the day wasn't far off when she would become my go-to person in several aspects of life—the most important was in making my body healthier than it had been in years. It was so exciting to think that we might finally be able to get this pain to a manageable level. It could not be cured, so this was about the best I could have hoped for. By the time I met Lauren, it had been eleven years of trying different treatments since my accident, and nothing had worked.

If the past few pages have had any "theme," I would have to say it was a refusal to give up no matter what. This was my health for the rest of my life I was talking about; I had to be dedicated, devoted, committed, and relentless. I had to learn to be my own advocate and I had done that.

Without even being conscious of it, my advocacy skills that I had taught myself during my medical struggles were enhancing the ones that I would eventually be using in my volunteer role as a victim advocate and eventually in my job. As I write that now, I am not sure whether that is an ironic coincidence, or if my medical advocacy led me to the field of victim advocacy as a natural progression.

Chapter 41
The Role of the Advocate

When we describe the role of an advocate, whether it is for victims of sexual or domestic violence, that of a medical advocate, an advocate to help you navigate through the legal system, or an advocate in a more general capacity, there are some specific characteristics or traits that are needed. I encourage you to be aware both of the qualities you need to strive for, and of your own self-care needs so you can remain emotionally healthy while pursuing this role.

The great list below, compiled by David Susman. Ph.D., appears on his "Advocating for Better Mental Health" website (*davidsusman.com*).

Ten Qualities of an Exceptional Advocate

1. **They are passionate.**
   Enthusiastic, driven, compassionate, caring. All of these characteristics convey the passion of exceptional advocates. Their work is more than a job requirement or a professional responsibility. It's a call and a lifelong mission.

2. **They are well informed.**
   Great advocates are often the most knowledgeable people in the room (region, state, nation) in their area of focus. They are continually learning, plugged into current streams of information, and always ready to share their knowledge and expertise to educate others.

3. **They are great communicators.**
   Whether expressing themselves verbally, in writing, and regardless of the medium (print, video, social channels), these amazing advocates communicate clearly, persuasively and respectfully to share information, viewpoints, and to advocate their mission.

4. **They are goal oriented.**
   Without a clear goal, there is no clear focus and no clear path forward. Exceptional advocates have laser-sharp goals, whether it is passing certain legislation, creating new programs, or garnering support for worthy causes.

5. **They are connectors.**
   Great advocates seem to have connections everywhere, with stakeholders at all levels. They are adept at building partnerships and coalitions and in connecting people with useful resources. They are often the first person people go to for information, support and advice.

6. **They are flexible.**
   The most effective advocates know the power of collaboration and compromise. Not every battle can be won. Sometimes small victories are the only road to eventual success. These advocates know that flexibility is essential in moving steadily forward to achieve their longer-term goals.

7. **They are inspiring.**
   What does it mean to be inspiring? It's hard to articulate, but great advocates move us, and they stir our thoughts and feelings. They give us hope for a brighter tomorrow and they outline a path for how we can reach it.

8. **They are empowering.**
   The best advocates not only inspire us, but they also instill in us a desire to pitch in and help out to collectively achieve a worthwhile goal. They show us how to raise our own voices to be heard and how to help others to find their voice. They also remind us that we all matter, and we all have a part to play.

9. **They are persistent.**
   Advocacy is not a sprint, it's a marathon. Important goals can take years or decades to achieve. Great advocates show up and keep showing up. They are not deterred by setbacks or disappointment. They are the first to arrive and the last to leave.

10. **They are servants.**
    In their hearts, great advocates are public servants. They do their work not for glory or fame, but for the quiet satisfaction of helping others and the steadfast belief that the work is the right thing to do and the only thing to do.

"While most of us may not reach the level of these exceptional advocates, we can certainly follow their example and try to learn how to use some of these same qualities in our own advocacy work," Susman says. "And remember, you don't have to be exceptional, you just have to have a desire to make a difference and a willingness to put in a little work and effort toward your goals. Let's get started."

TESTIMONIALS

I have set aside this section at the end of the book for testimonials from people who have known me for a variety of periods of time and in a number of different capacities. Some are lifelong peers or colleagues, who have been witness to how advocacy became an essential part of my life.

∿∿∿∿∿∿∿∿∿∿∿

Knowing Karen Hargrave since 2011 both personally and professionally, I can say that her moral values and character do not waver in either category, which gives her the foundation to be an advocate in life. Whether Karen is advocating for herself, her family, or her profession, her compassion, dedication, and openness are only a few of the qualities that are what I see when listening to her speak. As an advocate for her own well-being, she investigates all possibilities to obtain optimum health. I know this as a health care professional that has helped Karen navigate a few orthopedic health concerns over the past thirteen years when conventional medicine has left her with no solidified answers. This fierceness to find answers and solutions translates into every fiber of her responsibilities and accomplishments as an advocate for survivors of domestic violence and sexual abuse.

Karen is a comforting presence for survivors of any form of abuse, shown by her ability to be able to read the needs of those she is supporting. Whether it be sitting quietly waiting for the survivor to talk, cry, scream, or laugh, Karen is there like a chameleon ready and willing to change colors to fit the situation. An ear to listen, a shoulder to cry on, a tissue to be handed, a hand to lend, or guidance to see the strength within those who cannot see it within themselves … Karen is always there to support those who are unable to stand up or speak for themselves.

Not only does she advocate for each survivor individually, but Karen has also been a servant to the community for as long as I have known her. She worked for an agency that advocates for and serves victims of domestic and sexual violence in the city where we both lived. Although she left the organization to pursue other endeavors, her untiring desire for justice never left her soul.

Although I have personally been through a situation of domestic abuse prior to my knowing Karen, sharing my experience with her taught me a great deal of what it takes to be an advocate. Karen's selflessness is demonstrated by giving her time, resources, and education to prevent further abuse in any form. I had received help from a women's shelter and counseling during my ordeal. However, when you are in a place of fear and trepidation, the only focus is survival. This type of instinct is a moment-to-moment existence therefore one does not realize the skills of the advocate. It was only when I had far surpassed my tribulation that I met Karen and had the clear mind to realize her gift of advocacy.

It takes a very special person to be an advocate. I cannot say enough to give Karen the accolades she deserves.

— Lauren S. Felice, BA, LMT, BCTMB, NCCPT

Karen Hargrave was the volunteer coordinator during the time of our affiliation with an agency that served victims of sexual and domestic violence. My husband served as board president for many years, and I served as a foundation trustee, as a staff member and on various committees at different times. We remember her as a ball of positive energy and extremely thorough and passionate about her position and the organization's broader mission of ending domestic violence and sexual assault. Volunteers were a critical piece of the organization's mission fulfillment, and Karen went above and beyond in her efforts to train, develop, and nurture them.

Years later after we had all left the agency for various reasons, it had become obvious that mission drift led to poor hiring decisions, threatening the organization's safe services to its clients in the community, and putting at risk critical government and community funding sources. Due to her relentlessly passionate mission advocacy, Karen (from thousands of miles away in another state no less) took on an unofficial community leadership role by speaking out, rallying supporters, writing letters, creating posters, marching in front of the facility (she flew into town to do so) and speaking to the press in an effort to demand organizational transparency and accountability, oust the current agency's leadership, and "right the ship" as they say. With Karen's and others' advocacy efforts, we succeeded. We are forever grateful for Karen and her relentless advocacy for victims of domestic violence and sexual assault.

— Mark and Polly

Karen Hargrave exemplifies the definition of "advocate," no matter the cause. She is tireless in her efforts, refusing to take no for an answer, and coming to the defense of anyone who can use her help. In the years that I've known her, Karen has advocated for numerous causes—domestic violence, sexual assault, and medical issues, to name a few. Her empathy and unflagging patience make her resilient when supporting others as they endure traumatic situations. She has a truly special ability to keep other's best interests at heart; to listen and understand, and to consider situations from others' points of view.

— Christine Goodman

To describe Karen Hargrave the word warrior comes to mind. She is the ultimate advocate who can be as fierce as you need her to be at that moment. Be it up against a school nurse or going on camera to defend the mission of an agency where she used to work, who has now betrayed the people they set out to serve. You'd be lucky to have Karen Hargrave advocating for you at any given moment, and even luckier to call her friend.

— Kathy J.

Karen has a strong moral compass, fiercely and tirelessly advocating for others with passion, conviction, wisdom, and love. Whether it be for a victim of sexual assault, domestic violence, (diabetes/medical) awareness, or work ethic, Karen strives to make the world a better place for all. It has been my honor to have served with Karen as a volunteer advocate and now as a lifelong friend.

— Marcia Bellinger

I have known Karen for only a short time, less than three years actually. By the grace of God, we became neighbors in the fall of 2021. But it wasn't until my husband's passing in September 2022 that I got to experience the authenticity and compassionate heart of this woman, whose soul is on fire to make a difference in the lives of those who are hurting. The day after he passed away, Karen delivered enough homemade ziti with sauce, Caesar salad with all the fixings, and brownies extraordinaire to feed seven of us for days! That kindness and her other blessed offerings, too many to count, have shown me who Karen really is.

As a result of getting to know her and knowing I could trust her, we began sharing pieces of our lives with each other. She was easy to talk to, empathetic and understanding. When I found out what she had gone through with her car accident and her ongoing physical difficulties, I saw a strong woman. But when she revealed her son's medical struggles even to the point of educating others about them, I saw a determined woman. One who set out to turn those trials into opportunities and advocate for others with similar needs in similar situations.

When I learned how she had helped the domestic violence and sexual abuse victims at the agency in her community, I was extremely impressed. But I was even more impressed with what she did, after having moved away from that area and then learning that the agency had had a convicted sex offender working there for over two years. Karen's fierce, moral and ethical doctrine, and relentless gift of advocacy for victims, took on a life of its own. It fueled her righteous fire even more. Her determination to right that wrong did not rest until the sex offender was removed from the agency. Karen was definitely a force to be reckoned with.

Whether the person who came to her for help was a victim of abuse she met at the agency, a friend who didn't know where to turn, a family member who was hiding a secret out of fear, or just someone who needed a hug or an encouraging word, all of them came to Karen knowing they could trust her and she would help them. Karen's fortitude and experience in advocating for every one of them has definitely changed their lives for the better. Karen has a unique gift from God. She instinctively knows what someone needs, she knows what she can do to right their ship, expose the lies or cover-ups and stop the abuse in its tracks.

It is her mission to stop the hurt from continuing or from ever happening again. She is compelled in her role as an advocate to educate the uninformed and the misinformed as well as to help heal the broken and the hurting. This is Karen's God-given purpose and He has equipped her well. I know her book will be a blessing to many who are just getting to know the amazing gifts Karen has to offer and is thankfully willing to share.

— Carol J.

Our beautiful daughter has been in therapy to manage her feelings about being sexually abused. She also has Karen. Karen is "life support" for our daughter. She is a true advocate to help our daughter find her voice and strength. When you're a victim of sexual abuse, not everyone, including family members, will believe you and some will claim you are crazy. The believers and the non-believers. And of course, you must choose a side.

Karen has helped Ellen to share her truth, unwaveringly supporting her through the trauma.

How do you know you need an advocate to speak for you? You can't see clearly. You look up and all you see is the bottom. Our daughter was broken, and we were brokenhearted. We couldn't "fix" this.

Just imagine a special someone believes you. Helps you speak your truth. Supports you no matter what. Even when the rest of the world is against you.

I pray that if you need a special someone, you find someone like Karen.

— Greg and Barb

For the ten years I have known Karen, she has been a champion of helping those who need it most. As Karen's health coach, I have had the privilege of watching Karen be a proponent for her own health and the well-being of others.

Karen provides a listening ear, a shoulder to cry on, and a voice to the voiceless. She has helped countless victims of domestic and sexual abuse through her work at an agency whose mission serves these individuals. As you will learn in her book, her advocacy didn't stop after she left her position at this agency. Karen is an excellent role model on how to advocate for your own physical, emotional, and medical health in addition to providing support to those who may need it.

— Nick Leader

I can think of no one I know who would be a better author of a book about being an advocate than Karen Hargrave. I had the privilege and honor of sharing an office and working alongside Karen for years. I witnessed her skills and abilities advocating for victims of violence, as well as for her family.

— Dotti

Having known Karen Hargrave for the past twenty-five years, I can attest to her skills as a passionate and dedicated spokesperson for those who are unwilling or unable to advocate for themselves.

When her young son was diagnosed with a life-threatening medical condition, she worked tirelessly with sometimes unenlightened school personnel to assure that his medical and social needs were being met. Karen's determination to advocate for her child's cause ensured that the road to proper oversight for children with similar needs would be more easily navigated by families in the future.

As her children grew older, she became a volunteer, and then a paid staff member, at a local domestic violence agency; in her role working at the agency, she was a tireless spokesperson for women who had lost their voice to advocate for themselves. She extended her advocacy from afar after moving to another state, when she recognized decisions had been made at her former workplace which were not in the best interest of the victims she had served. She led a successful charge which challenged those decisions, resulting in a change of leadership.

— Jan G.

I have had the privilege of knowing Karen for over two decades. I have always admired Karen's creativity and her willingness to expand her skills and knowledge by learning new crafting techniques. In addition to being an incredibly talented artist, Karen is also one of the strongest, most courageous, caring, and loyal women I know. She is not afraid to advocate for a cause she believes in and will offer support and guidance to those who ask for her help. On a personal level, throughout the years of our friendship, she has helped me navigate through some difficult situations with my extended family. I will always be grateful for her support. I am truly blessed to have Karen as a friend.

— Beth H.

Karen has been instrumental in helping me navigate an exceedingly difficult family situation. Her professionalism, compassion, advocacy, and empathy have been (and continue to be) much-needed comforts through a very trying time.

— Christopher

I admire anyone who has the conviction to champion for themselves and for others. Karen Hargrave has intuitively learned the value of advocating not only for her own needs but for others who may not have the skills or freedom to speak for themselves. Her unyielding sense of morality has made her a staunch spokesperson for many and has helped guide countless people towards action and hopefully towards healing. As a health care provider of 43 years who's been a witness to many victims of all sorts of trauma, I know how valuable that type of support can be for one's human spirit. It is incumbent on each of us to follow her example to help our fellow humans. Well done, Karen, and thank you.

—*Renée Mooney RN DC*

RESOURCES
FOR SURVIVORS OF SEXUAL AND DOMESTIC VIOLENCE

NATIONWIDE

Rape Abuse Incest National Network (RAINN)
www.rainn.org | (800) 656-HOPE

*RAINN offers an online hotline, which
can be accessed via phone or online chat*

Joyful Heart Foundation
www.joyfulheartfoundation.org | (212) 475-2026

National Domestic Violence Hotline
www.thehotline.org | (800) 799-7233

National Coalition Against Domestic Violence
www.ncadv.org
*This agency DOES NOT provide client services,
but is a vast resource of services that are currently available*

LOCAL TO NASSAU COUNTY
& JACKSONVILLE, FL

Micah's Place Fernandina Beach, Florida
www.micahsplace.org | (904) 225-9979

Hubbard House Jacksonville, Florida
www.hubbardhouse.org | (904) 354-3114

Women's Center of Jacksonville, Florida
www.thewcj.org | (904) 722-3000

*Most domestic violence and sexual assault hotlines offer a "quick escape"
option, so survivors can visit their site without worrying about their
abuser tracking their online activity.*

ACKNOWLEDGEMENTS

I would like to sincerely thank the following people for their contributions to this book.

I could not have done it without you, and I appreciate your contribution so much!

- Kevin Hargrave
- Michelle
- Lauren S. Felice
- Mary Lee
- Katie
- Lynn and Devynn
- Lauren Marie
- Chris
- Jen
- Emily
- Christopher
- Maggie Mercer
- Kelly Downey
- Carol J.
- Barb
- Tammy
- Dotti
- Everyone who wrote a testimonial for the book

CONTRIBUTORS

Grace Robin Evans
Christopher
Lauren S. Felice
Katie
Mary Lee
Lauren Marie
Lynn & Devynn
Jen
Chris
Kevin Hargrave
Maggie Mercer
Carol J.
Kelly Downey

AUTHOR'S PAGE

Karen Hargrave found her calling in advocacy through early life-changing events. It greatly influenced who she is as a person and as an advocate. It inspired her passion for advocacy, which grew throughout her life and continues to grow to this day.

Karen grew up in Central New York and pursued an education focused on art and psychology. She graduated from Nazareth College in 1991 with a B.S. in studio art and a minor in psychology. She completed a master's level clinical program in art therapy at Hillside Children's Center in Rochester, New York. Hillside is a residential treatment facility for children and teens who have experienced abuse and trauma. She completed her master's degree in human services counseling through Oswego State University, and she worked briefly as a therapist before staying home to raise her children.

Karen's husband, Kevin Hargrave, was employed as a state trooper, and together they raised two sons in Baldwinsville, New York. Karen began volunteering at an agency that served victims of sexual and domestic violence. She eventually was hired for the staff position of coordinating and supervising the volunteers who responded to sexual assault calls to area hospitals. This involved crisis intervention and support for recent victims of sexual assault. Karen recruited, trained, and supervised the volunteers who responded to these calls, as well as responding to calls herself. Karen and Kevin relocated when Kevin retired and now live in Fernandina Beach, Florida.

APPENDIX

The Science Behind PTSD: How Trauma Changes the Brain

The section below is taken from *Psych Central.com*, a website on mental health issues:

After any type of trauma, the brain and body can change. When we experience trauma, our brains do not function normally. Our brains direct all our mental and physical energy towards dealing with the immediate threat until it is gone. In normal situations, this state fades away over time. Trauma isn't just something we experience after being in a war zone or a violent situation, we can be traumatized by our relationships. Sometimes our initial trauma response sticks, making it difficult for us to function normally.

Trauma can change the way that we think, feel and act for a long time after the initial event. It has a permanent effect on us. For many people, this can mean flashbacks or nightmares, a constant feeling of being on edge, loneliness, anger, intrusive thoughts and memories, self-destructive actions and more. All of these things are normal responses to trauma, but they do not always go away on their own. The good news is that although these patterns seem permanent, they can actually be reversed. With the right approach, techniques, and knowledge, you can shift your brain towards healing. It is easiest to first understand how and why these changes are happening.

There are 3 parts of the brain: the amygdala, the prefrontal cortex and the hippocampus. The effects of trauma go after several areas of your brain at once. All three parts work together to manage stress. When you are reminded of a traumatic experience, your amygdala (emotional and survival center) goes into overdrive, acting just as it would if you were experiencing the trauma for the first time. Your prefrontal cortex also becomes suppressed, so you are less capable of controlling your fear—you are stuck in a purely reactive state. Simultaneously, trauma also leads to reduced activity in the hippocampus, one of whose functions is to distinguish between the past and present. In other words, your brain can't tell the difference between the actual traumatic event and the memory of it. It perceives things that trigger memories as threats themselves. Trauma can cause your brain to remain in the state of hypervigilance, suppressing your memory and impulse control, and trapping you in a constant state of strong emotional activity.

Our brains are extremely adaptable. The brain's ability to form new connections explains why we can rewire our brains to reverse the trauma's damaging effects. Our brains are more susceptible to change than many people think and even though overcoming trauma is very difficult, you're actually changing the way your brain works. You are adding new pathways, increasing the functions of certain areas, and strengthening connections. This is the same mechanism that allows us to grow and change by learning.

During the healing process you can actually rewire and retrain your brain to reverse the effects of trauma. You can reinforce your prefrontal cortex and get back rationality and control; you can strengthen your hippocampus and help your memory work how it is supposed to work. You can even subdue the hyperactive amygdala which will help bring you peace with time and therapeutic methods along with the right kind of help you can find a way to overcome trauma right down to your neurons. (Psych Central, 2024).

BIBLIOGRAPHY

Children's Assessment Center. CACHouston.org,
https://cachouston.org. February 18, 2024.

Domestic Abuse Intervention Programs: Home of the Duluth Model.
https://www.theduluthmodel.org. February 19, 2024.

EMDR Institute Inc. emdr.com,
https://www.emdr.com.

Finkelhor, D. (1994). The international epidemiology of child sexual
abuse. *Child Abuse & Neglect*, 18(5), 409-417.

ImRoc. Imroc.org,
https://imroc.org. February 22, 2024.

Joyful Heart Foundation
https://www.joyfulheart.com. February 18, 2024.

KMD Law.
https://www.kmdlaw.com.

McNeil, Liz. *A Rape, A Reckoning, A Renewal.* People Magazine,
January 22, 2024. pgs. 39-45.

National Domestic Violence Hotline.
https://www.thehotline.org. February 18, 2024.

National Institute of Mental Health.
https://www.nimh.nih.gov. *How Can I Take Care of my Mental
Health?* February 14, 2024.

Niskanen, Noora. EMDR/Trauma Therapy,
https://www.nooraniskanen.com

Psych Central,
https://psychcentral.com.

Psychology Today.
https://www.psychologytoday.com. March 17, 2009.

Repper, J. & Perkins, R (2003) *Social Inclusion and Recovery.* Balliere Tindall, [Google Scholar]

Rape, Abuse, Incest National Network (RAINN) https://www.rainn.org. February 18, 2024.

Sedlak, A.J., Mettenburg, J., Basena, M., Petta, I., McPherson, K., Greene, A., and Li, S. (2010), *Fourth National Incidence Study of Child Abuse and Neglect (NIS-4):* Report to Congress, Washington, DC: US Department of Health & Human Services, Administration for Child and Families.

Shepherd, G., Boardman, J. & Slade, M. (2008) *Making Recovery a Reality.* Policy Paper. Sansbury Centre for Mental Health [Google Scholar].

Susman, David, PhD. *Advocating for Better Mental Health.* https://www.davidsusman.com. February 14, 2024.

The lotus flower is a symbol of overcoming adversity through life's challenges. Lotus flowers are most commonly found in swampy, difficult terrain. So, they symbolize the idea that out of ugliness, destruction and unrest, we can all come together and emerge from the dark murky water, pristine and beautiful.